The Inner World of the School
Children's Ideas about Schools

Cedric Cullingford

CASSELL

Cassell Educational Limited
Villiers House
41/47 Strand
London WC2N 5JE

First published 1991

British Library Cataloguing in Publication Data
Cullingford, Cedric
    The inner world of the school: children's ideas about
    schools. — (Children, teachers and learning series)
    1. School life. Attitude of students
    I. Title   II. Series
    371.81

Typeset by Litho Link Ltd., Welshpool, Powys
Printed and bound in Great Britain by Biddles Ltd., Guildford and
King's Lynn

ISBN 0-304-32365-9 (hardback)
        0-304-32366-7 (paperback)

Contents

For William Percival

Foreword

The books in this series stem from the conviction that all those who are concerned with education should have a deep interest in the nature of children's learning. Teaching and policy decisions ultimately depend on an understanding of individual personalities accumulated through experience, observation and research. Too often in recent years decisions on the management of education have had little to do with the realities of children's lives, and too often the interest shown in the performance of teachers, or in the content of the curriculum, has not been balanced by an interest in how children respond to either. The books in this series are based on the conviction that children are not fundamentally different from adults, and that we understand ourselves better by our insight into the nature of children.

The books are designed to appeal to *all* those who are interested in education and take it as axiomatic that anyone concerned with human nature, culture or the future of civilization is interested in education; in the individual process of learning, as well as what can be done to help it. While each book draws on recent findings in research, and is aware of the latest developments in policy, each is written in a style that is clear, readable and free from the jargon that has undermined much scholarly writing, especially in such a relatively new field of study.

Although the audience to be addressed includes all those concerned with education, the most important section of the audience is made up of professional teachers, the teachers who continue to learn and grow and who need both support and stimulation. Teachers are very busy people, whose energies are taken up in coping with difficult circumstances. They deserve material that is stimulating, useful and free of jargon and that is in tune with the practical realities of classrooms.

Each book is based on the principle that the study of education is a discipline in its own right. There was a time when the study of the principles of learning and the individual's response to his or her environment was a collection of parts of other disciplines — history, philosophy, linguistics, sociology and psychology. That time is assumed to be over and the books address those who are interested in the study of children and how they respond to their environment. Each book is written both to enlighten the reader and to offer practical help to develop understanding. They therefore not only contain accounts of what we understand about children, but also illuminate these accounts by a series of examples, based on observation of practice. These examples are designed not as a series of rigid steps to be followed, but to show the realities on which the insights are based.

Most people, even educational researchers, agree that research on children's learning has been most disappointing, even when it has not been completely missing. Apart from the general lack of a 'scholarly' educational tradition, the inadequacies of such study come about because of the fear of approaching such a complex area as children's inner lives. Instead of answering curiosity with observation, much educational research has attempted to reduce the problem to simplistic solutions, by isolating a particular hypothesis and trying to prove it, or by trying to focus on what is easy and 'empirical'. These books try to clarify the real complexities of the problem, and are willing to be speculative. The real disappointment with educational research, however, is that it is very rarely read or used. The people most at home with children are often unaware that helpful insights can be offered to them. The study of children and the understanding that comes from self-knowledge are too important to be left to obscurity. In the broad sense real 'research' is carried out by all those engaged in the task of teaching or bringing up children.

All the books share a conviction that the inner worlds of children repay close attention, and that much subsequent behaviour and attitudes depend upon the early years. The books also share the conviction that children's natures are not markedly different from those of adults, even if they are more honest about themselves. The process of learning is reviewed as the individual's close and idiosyncratic involvement in events, rather than the passive reception of, and processing of, information.

Cedric Cullingford

CHAPTER 1

Introduction: The Ethos of School

'Why do I come to school? Because I have to.'

Everyone is an expert on their own education, for learning is a personal matter. And yet education is also an institutional matter on which many people have opinions. Once the subject is made a public matter rather than a personal experience, it is discussed in very different terms. The stress is on outcomes, on what can be measured and tested, on organization and efficiency. Viewed as a system it is easy to see education in simple terms. The subjects to be taken are prescribed and the levels of attainment set. The broad and balanced curriculum is delivered and, to make sure it is learned, meticulously assessed. But the moment parts of the system are tested we discover that the realities of the school experience are not quite so simple.

From our own memories we realize that the process of learning is a complex one. It is difficult for us to know when and where, let alone why, we learned, and forgot, certain facts and different skills, where our attitudes were welded and how our prejudices formed. We do know that learning was not a simple matter of listening, that we were confronted with subjects that filled us with distaste as well as those we pursued with enthusiasm. We are also aware of the significance of different teachers; each one influencing, positively or negatively, in a subtle way. If we apply our own insight into individual learning we realize that the realities of school for each child are a complex matter. We acknowledge differences in motivation, enthusiasm, support from parents and friends, and learning styles. It is awareness of these individual differences that mark out the best teachers. One can lead the child to the curriculum but one cannot make him learn.

The desire to learn and to understand begins so early that it must be considered natural, but this desire does not last undiminished through the years of schooling. This, in itself, should give pause for thought. But discussions about the curriculum, and about management of schools, rarely take children into account. All the areas of controversy, whether it is about the contents of a syllabus or its style, like 'facts' and 'empathy' as the motivating force in learning history, are explored from any point of view except that of the learner, as if all responsibility were over once the syllabus was set. But every teacher recognizes the differences between what is taught and what is learned.

Children have a natural curiosity. The desire to learn is allied to a discriminating sense of what is being expected of them. Their insights into the nature of schooling are revealing and deserve to be taken into account. Children are not just the recipients of the curriculum, but have clear ideas about what is successful in its delivery. They are the ones who are most closely interested in matters of discipline and school organization. Their clear and articulate views can give us insights into what it is like to be in school, and how well schools are working. Our own memories fade, and we rely on anecdote. The children who are in schools reveal their shared experiences in a way that has important implications. This is not only because of the insights children offer about their learning, or because they are revealing an area of their inner worlds which is rarely explored. It is because their statements have implications on policy, on how schools are organized, and how teachers manage their classrooms.

Children reveal that they have the articulateness and honesty to analyse what they experience. They show consistent judgement and evidence for what they are saying. Their views deserve to be taken into account because they know, better than anyone, which teaching styles are successful, which techniques of learning bring the best out of them, and what the ethos of the school consists of. The evidence that has been collected from children deals with many of the most central and important questions. What are schools for? What is the purpose of the education system? Are our present policies working? Listening to children makes us reconsider some of the habits we have taken for granted.

The evidence taken from the children has been organized into central themes, but there are certain questions which are addressed throughout. It is worth being aware of some of these questions in reading the evidence, for they have bearings on many of the most controversial issues.

What is the nature of the curriculum? How much of what is learned is 'hidden', consisting of ideas that are implied rather than clearly stated? Do children acquire certain attitudes from the teachers that have a bearing on their behaviour and attitudes to society? Are skills more important than the acquisition of knowledge? Are some subjects given much more weight than others and therefore taken more seriously? What is the purpose that underlies all parts of the curriculum? Do they all have the same purpose or are some not to be taken too seriously? Does the curriculum that is envisaged as 'broad and balanced', including music and physical education, strike children that way?

What is the distinction between formal and informal learning? Is any teaching style 'informal' to a pupil? How much use should teachers make of group work? Are the most successful lessons those with a great deal of content, carefully organized? Do children need to learn certain things by themselves? How free should children be to learn in their own way? Do they prefer teachers to be distant or personally friendly?

What does 'child-centredness' mean? Do children expect to be cajoled into learning? What is the place of 'topic' work in the minds of pupils? Are 'discovery' methods the most beneficial? What exactly is 'time on task'? Does it indicate that when children are busy they are also learning? What helps children understand concepts? How much of the time are children engaged in useful activities? Is every moment well spent? How much do they learn from each other? How much time is spent waiting for something to happen? What do children expect of school in terms of discipline?

All these issues are not addressed in government reports. The curriculum, the question of discipline and the management of schools are not only experienced but analysed by children. The evidence in this book reveals how clearly children express their points of view on all these issues. And their opinions deserve to be taken into account. We learn about successful teaching, about the organization of classes, about sensible discipline, and about the environment of the school. And we also learn about the personal experience of the formative years of life.

Schools are very particular institutions. Each one has its own culture. But like each individual, they have a lot in common with each other. We might be able to detect (or believe we can detect) the ethos of each school as we walk in; but we must also remember that in the context of the large community, each school is very similar. Each school has its place. The experience of those who have been to school is both unique *and* a common experience, although, it must be admitted, the evidence presented comes from day schools in the public sector rather than from private boarding schools. It would, however, be surprising if the daily experience of school as presented here were alien to anyone.

All experiences are both private and public. Felt personally, they are nevertheless shared. The children who describe their own circumstances in these pages come from a variety of backgrounds. The schools, of course, like the children, remain anonymous; as do those teachers who were so helpful in the gathering of information. But the experience of school for all pupils, whatever their peculiar circumstances, whether from a part of London where the majority of inhabitants come from ethnic minorities, or a part of the country where their parents are commonly farmers, is a homogeneous one. Each emotion experienced, whether dread or joy, disappointment or excitement, is both private and common. Out of this account of the actual experience of schools we build a picture of what schools are really like.

CHAPTER 2

Children's Individual and Collective Experience

'I think teachers are a good thing but I think we can help each other.'

Children are the centre and purpose of a large industry. A significant proportion of a nation's budget is spent on the building and running of schools, the purchase of books and equipment and the employment of teachers. In addition there are, more obscurely devoted to children's service, large government departments and local bureaucracies. All these are in addition to parents becoming more closely involved in their children's education.

The amount of resources involved in education is so great it is, perhaps, not surprising that many are tempted to treat the education system as an industry. To them what counts is the quality of the product. Although some of the more marked analogies between schools and production lines are clearly inappropriate, the tendency to see education in terms of outcomes — so many qualifications as against so much financial investment — is understandable. This means that children, as raw material or finished product, are seen in a particular light.

Similar measurements of success or failure are applied to any number of institutions and people. Appraisal of performance with sharply measured outcomes is part of the culture of the day. And yet no one would assert that their own inner life could be weighed in this way. We might all make general judgements on each other and justify such assertions by examples. We might like the precision that seems to be denoted by performance indicators, and we will recognize the crucial distinction between financial failure and success. But the most powerful examples of human achievement are measured in more difficult terms. Of all 'indicators' it is quality that is most difficult to measure; which does not mean that it can be ignored, or that it is not worth worrying about. And quality depends more on communication than anything else.

Formal appraisals are desires to communicate feelings and

judgements more objectively. However insights are derived, they all have to be expressed. Each individual, after all, is judged by words as well as actions, for each one defines himself by language. 'I have to use words when I'm talking to you.' The ability to communicate what we think and feel, at whatever level, is what creates each person's individuality. The ability to understand other people's communication is what creates the relationship of oneself to the world.

The reason that the need to understand one's own and other people's language is being insisted upon is that we appear to forget that children are also human. Despite their personal feelings and ideas, their intelligence and their insights, and despite their centrality to the education system, children are rarely listened to. They are measured and appraised, observed and cajoled, but when it comes to research, rarely questioned. Why?

One answer must lie in an ancient sense of egotism in adults. We know so much more than children and can explain so much more precisely that children are, in contrast, limited. This leads to an unexamined assumption that children do not really know what they think, and that they are so busy taking in information that all we can do is measure the amount they have imbibed. The fact that children think intelligently and examine their circumstances constantly is proven.[1] But it is still difficult to take in the implications of the fact.

Even if children are recognized as having ideas of their own, there is another myth which prevents them being taken seriously. This is the assumption that what children say cannot be trusted, that they are either so lazy they cannot be bothered to articulate the whole truth, or they are trying so hard to please that they guess what the questioner wants to hear. As in the case of adults being asked for their opinions, there is a danger in over-simplification. But children have two advantages in interviews. They do not know what the norm of expectation is. They can be disconcerting because they are not yet imbued with shared social certainties. And children have not developed the art of self-deception. Most of what people say, however great their deliberate mendacity, is true.[2] In children's cases, they have not discovered good reasons why this should not be so.

The most significant explanation of the absence of children from research, however, lies in the view of them as subjects. The tradition in educational research, until recently, has been based, with notable exceptions, on the semi-scientific method of proving an hypothesis. For the sake of complete objectivity it is important to cut out as many variables as possible. And nothing could have more variables than language, which reflects the complexity of the human mind. Actions observed in different conditions seem to carry more weight than what goes on inside the mind. But these methods of research also suggest the need for a hypothesis to test. This means that the researcher will have a point to make already formulated. He will have needed to have made a number of assumptions about the children, their age, their gender, their ethnic origin or their social class in order to narrow down on the variables and give respectable statistical proof.

Against the precision of a scientific experiment, often repeated to test its consistent legitimacy, the human mind is a complex, ungainly, difficult instrument. The most direct way to explore children's thinking is through language. But this implies an approach in contrast to the need to isolate variables. It means listening to what children say, exploring with them what matters, indeed, deliberately avoiding them knowing what it is that the questioner *wishes* them to say. To interview children is to avoid having hypotheses, to allow them to define what is significant. Of course we are clear about the subject that is being discussed, but we make no assumptions about what children should say. At the heart of ethnographic research is the belief that it is what goes on *inside* the mind that is most significant. Interviews with psychoanalysts go to the heart of what people think, even subconsciously, and are taken as real evidence. Interviews which explore what people think are far less superficial than simple questionnaires that try to force people into replying 'yes' or 'no'.

The research for this book is based on lengthy semi-structured interviews. The way that the research is presented is not through statistical analysis, as the significant findings create a coherent picture that is consistent. The quotations taken from the children are there to illuminate the carefully documented findings. To quote from a similar study:

... These *are* systematic studies. Although I have used quotations and examples to illustrate the children's growing understanding, they are not simply anecdotes ... Rather the examples serve to support conclusions from careful documented study.[3]

The material that illustrates what children say could be repeated again and again. Each individual will use his or her own language, but a message such as 'the purpose of schools is to prepare us for jobs' is one that is all pervasive. The interviews are there to give children the chance to explore issues that matter to them.

Children in this survey spoke freely and openly about their feelings and ideas without trying to please or shock the interviewer. They were able to analyse clearly what they experience and were quick to give supporting evidence for what they were saying. They were aware of the distinction between rumour and fact. They acknowledged what a strong hold rumour and anecdote have on their picture of the world, just as they have on adult attitudes. Given the privacy of the interview, children were very open about what they said and did not show any tendency to cover up or be obscure. Children might show an occasional desire not to be bothered with answering a question — 'I don't know' — but this did not manifest itself in these interviews about a subject that clearly interests and concerns them, and about which they might talk at length to their peers, but rarely to an adult. What children say is the clearest and most revealing insight into their minds.

All the interviews were carried out using a tape-recorder (put to one side and quickly forgotten) and lasted about one hour. They were semi-structured in the sense of having certain topics that would always be brought up, but open enough to be able to explore points that the children wished to take further, and to pursue the topics without any prearranged order. It is felt that a private interview with each child is far more useful, if more time-consuming, than a general group discussion and that the presence of a teacher could inhibit what they were saying. After a possible shyness lasting a minute or two all the children soon got into their stride. The material is so abundant that only a small selection of it can appear. But more important than its abundance is its consistency.

Altogether 110 children were interviewed, divided equally

between those in their last year of primary school and their first year of secondary school. The children were a semi-random sample. This was random in taking a list of names from different classes and having an equal number of boys and girls, and selected only to the small extent of making sure that ethnic minorities, or disabled children, would be represented in the survey. Teachers were asked to ascertain, beforehand, that the children interviewed gave a broad reflection of different abilities and backgrounds, but this did not throw any extra light on the interviews except to confirm the consistency of pupils' responses. The teachers were always co-operative and did not demand that material should be given to them after the interviews.

Within the survey were four primary schools and three secondary schools, although some useful background work was carried out in other schools which is not cited in the quotations. The schools in the research were from a part of what was the Inner London Education Authority and from schools in a small South Midlands town, surrounded by countryside. Although the subject of the interviews was all about the experience of schools, of teachers and peer groups, authority and learning styles, the interviews were *ostensibly* about the transfer from primary to secondary school.[4]

The reason for this was to give no sense at all of what the interviews were seeking to contain. Transfer from one school to another is not only a moment of great salience for children but one which can easily justify the asking of questions. Direct questions of what they think of schools and their teachers, which they have become used to accept, *could* have run the danger of preventing the same freedom of talk. Once the immediate experience of transfer had become the starting point of the interviews children commented on a range of issues. The more they analysed their experience, the more they wished to say, as if they had had, at last, an opportunity to clarify their opinions. And the subject of transfer pointed up the differences between teachers and rules, styles of working and the curriculum.

Secondary children were able to compare their changed experiences against their expectations, and primary children were able to formulate all that they most feared, and most hoped for, in secondary schools. Whilst there was a clear unity in what was being said, primary and secondary school children revealed a slight shift in the style of their answers, as if the ethos of the different kinds of school makes its presence felt rapidly. Secondary school children showed a tendency to be more abrasive and laconic, as if they had learned to cope with a harsher reality.

The differences between primary and secondary schools are interesting and significant. But they also show the essential similarities in all kinds of schooling. The surroundings might be different, and the teachers play a different role. But from the children's points of view, similar rules and experiences remain. The age of transfer, from ten to eleven, lies at the heart of the formal experience of childhood. They are acknowledged to be half-way through their rite of passage to adulthood. They have become aware of some of the implications of the changes; the power of others, when powerless themselves, seeing both the unselfconsciousness of the very young and the growing awkwardness of adolescents. And that central fact of transfer is also of interest to their parents and their friends. No longer can they be ignored as they progress through the privacies of school. No longer can some of the ground rules of friendship remain untested.

Each individual child's unique interpretation of school is influenced by his parents, his early experiences and by his friends. Much of what is learned depends on the attitudes brought to bear on the work, on motivation and on confidence. Such attitudes are themselves formed by a variety of influences, from casual conversations as much as formal lecturing, from observed behaviour as much as instruction, from overheard remarks as much as lessons. Children learn what they want to, or rather avoid learning what they do not want to, and spend as much time analysing the peculiarities of the institution of which they are part as they do fulfilling the demands of lessons. The behaviour of teachers and other children all vary according to the temperament and characteristics of the individual child. Given all this, and the many possibilities for a great variety of responses, is it surprising how unified are the views expressed by children, and how similar are the assumptions held by different friendship groups?

The children in the schools themselves came from a variety of backgrounds, from virtually all the social permutations held as significant in analyses of this kind, except for children from backgrounds wealthy enough to send them to private schools. There were obviously gifted children and obviously slow ones, as one can see in their statements about themselves. Some children were clearly doing their best to conform to be good. Others were quite open about their deviousness, their tendency to get into trouble. And yet their views were homogeneous. There are shared assumptions about school that are characteristic despite differences in background. For all the surface variety and individual differences there must be something about the school as an institution which is pervasive. There are clear differences between primary and secondary schools, and between the success or failure of one school and another as there are between groups of teachers, but these differences do not prevent children expressing very similar attitudes, whatever school they are in.[5] An attempt to point out different characteristics, to make a vertical as well as a horizontal analysis, came to nothing. There were different approaches to school, and a few children who could be placed in a special category, but the unity of the underlying opinions was such that despite the obvious complexity of the response one could not label them into groups as one might perhaps label teachers.[6]

This unity of response is itself a significant finding. Children showed consistent attitudes towards their work whether they thought themselves successful at it or not. It seems important to draw out the general and shared assumptions about school before setting up an hypothesis based on differences in background. These interviews suggest there is a great deal of material in children's collective vision which needs to be explored. The interviews did not lend themselves to statistical analysis. When a statement begins, 'The children said . . .', it means just that. All the children agreed about major influences such as the purpose of schools. All children answered freely.[7] Once the material had been gathered the transcripts were reviewed to find what themes emerged. No pre-set hypotheses were being tested. The material was analysed several times, to discover what children were saying, and only then organized into the headings that now appear. There were many different ways in which the

11

transcriptions could have been structured, since there must be a great deal of overlap between, say, views of teachers and teaching styles, and their own learning styles. The important fact is that the evidence that emerged was not pre-judged. What emerged, therefore, was subject to careful analysis. All the major themes that mark out children's insights presented themselves. The question was how much repetitive evidence to give, and how to make sure that the actual quotations were as representative as possible. In all cases they are standard rather than eccentric, whatever the temptation to present the more bizarre of children's experiences. But the quotations also give the actual flavour of the individual point of view. Despite the clear and consistent findings that emerge there are also individual points of view. All statements which conclude 'children think that . . .' are, indeed, the summary of collective, individual opinions, without any collusion or collaboration.

Children spend a great deal of time in schools and they are one of the focal points in their lives. They do not clearly separate the life they lead at home from the one they lead in school (although they do not always like the intrusion of one world into the other). Many of their experiences, like friendship, are common to both. But children also see school as distinct. They not only carry their own rules but have a style of carrying out these rules which is all their own.

Children analyse the rules by which teachers run their schools. Teachers use language differently from other people. They reveal attitudes towards girls and boys which are different. Teachers are themselves carefully studied by the children in their care, for their friendliness or distance, for their ability to accept humour and for their ability to explain. Children reveal, unwittingly, how complex and difficult is the teacher's task. They also demonstrate many ways in which teachers can help children improve their work, through their attitudes to what they are doing, their belief in the children and their expectations of work. But teachers work in a difficult context. Children reveal many facets of their schooling that show a dichotomy between what teachers would like to achieve and what they can actually achieve in the circumstances. Given the circumstances, teachers generally do surprisingly well.

Nevertheless children implicitly question the circumstances. They are imbued with the expectations of their parents and the attitudes of their peer groups, as well as accepting, up to a point, the implied values of school. Many of the attitudes speak for themselves, but we should look at the evidence that children put forward to question what goes on in the schooling system as we know it. Do children really believe in schools? What do they learn about values and about the purpose of school? What do they learn about behaviour? What do they learn about authority? What are the learning styles they find most useful? Do they receive all they want to from their experience in the classroom? All these questions are addressed by what the children say, and the picture that emerges should give us the means to assess the kind of impact that school has on their lives. Children accept schools as they are, and do not automatically reject what goes on. But the atttitudes they express also inform them as future parents, and as people who look back on their own experience of schooling in a specific way. There are many distinctions between the ostensible values of school and those which children receive.

There is no reason to doubt what children say, for they are consistent in their judgements and, from a wide variety of backgrounds, agree about some of the fundamental experiences they undergo, both within and outside the classroom. In the end the importance of school lies in the individual experience of all those who are in it. What children say should help us understand better what that experience is, and lead us to reassess the nature of the provision. After all, the ultimate reality is that which is experienced by each individual.

NOTES AND REFERENCES

1. Cullingford, C. *The Nature of Learning*. London: Cassell, 1990.
2. J. L. Austin and other philosophers of language have, with all the suspicions of linguistic truth implicit in logical positivism, pointed out that at least 90 per cent of statements must be true.
3. Dunn, J. *The Beginnings of Social Understanding*. Oxford: Basil Blackwell, 1988, p. 3.
4. There have been a number of studies about transfer, e.g. Nisbet, J. D. and Entwistle, N. J. *The Transition to Secondary Education*. London: University of London Press, 1969; Spelman, B. J. *Pupil Adaptation to Secondary School*. Belfast: Northern Ireland Council for Education

Research, 1979; Galton, M. and Willcocks, J. *Moving from the Primary Classroom*. London: Routledge and Kegan Paul, 1983; but very few are concerned with the inner experience of children. Only L. Measor and P. Woods (*Changing Schools: Pupil Perspectives on Transfer to a Comprehensive*. Milton Keynes: Open University Press, 1984) studied the children's anxieties about size, discipline, demands on work, bullying and making and losing friends, all themes which emerge in their interviews.

5. Rutter, M., Maughan, B., Mortimore, P. and Ouston, J. *Fifteen Thousand Hours — Secondary Schools and Their Effects on Children*. London: Open Books, 1979. Mortimore, P., Sammons, P., Stoll, L., Lewis, D. and Ecob, R. *School Matters: The Junior Years*. Wells: Open Books, 1988.

6. Galton, M., Simon, B. and Croll, P. *Inside the Primary Classroom*. London: Routledge and Kegan Paul, 1980.

7. It should be noted that all transcripts have been reproduced verbatim, including grammatical errors.

CHAPTER 3
The Reputation of Schools

'We've heard about it on *Grange Hill* and that.'   (boy, secondary)

Schools are the first institutions we experience. Many of the assumptions people make, about the nature of work and authority, about formal relationships and formal language, derive from their experiences of school. But opinions about school are formed long before we first enter them. They are based on anticipation by the individual, expectation in the family and collective assumptions in the community. These assumptions are based not just on the rumours that circulate about different schools, but on the personal memories of each individual's experience of at least ten years' full-time schooling.

To parents, who have the most immediate interest in schools, much of what they observe remains arcane. Those practices of rules and regulations that once enclosed them become exclusive. The corridors and classrooms that were once their own are now closed to them. The obscure authority of the headteacher somehow remains intact. So parents accept the collective memory of schools, and their particular habits of presentation; the wall displays and territories used for curious purposes. It is not only parents who carry the collective vision of schools. The whole community will associate the local school with bustling corridors, crowded rooms and complex rules. Memory is selective and focuses not so much on the daily routine but on the traumatic or exciting moments, on shared escapades or isolated punishment, not so much on work as on the fear of bullying.

Most adults hold equivocal attitudes to school. Schools are places of work, with measures of success published as examination results. At the same time schools are places with an atmosphere all their own, places of tempestuous activity, and of eccentricity. A similar duality of attitude prevails in attitudes to teachers. They are, on the one hand, respected as people of authority. On the other hand they are often considered to do a job which is undemanding both in time and level. Little

15

professional status is granted to teachers, for the very dedication that drives them to work for so little remuneration is held in some suspicion. Why put up with such poor conditions of work? Those looking at schools easily come to the conclusion that teachers do what they do for obscure, possibly nefarious, purposes. Thus the essential fact of schools which affects all pupils — that they have no choice but *must* be there — also touches the teachers. If they had a choice *would* they be there?

Schools are essentially autonomous institutions. They stand out in the community landscape. They express their difference in their architecture and their collective values, in their rules and their functions. Even teachers have equivocal attitudes to schools. A significant proportion were themselves unhappy at school and entered the profession with a determination to do something about it. Many people share negative memories of school. In a number of surveys of young people's attitudes, it is clear that many were unhappy at school.[1] This is due not to isolated incidents such as bullying or unfairness, but to a sense of bewilderment about what it was all for. Those pupils who have not been successful enough to go on to higher education, and even many who have, feel that their own schooling lacked relevance and purpose. The curriculum seemed to have little to do with their subsequent lives. Looking back, ex-pupils wish that they had learned more of the skills they feel they lack. Even more tellingly, they feel that schools did not address central issues in the social and political environment in which they lived. They wondered about the purpose of schools.

Parents are, of course, ex-pupils. Part of the mystery of school remains with them; that there were secret rules and hidden purposes, of which only the teachers were aware. Although schools have a clear ostensible purpose that is rarely questioned, the way they carry out their purpose is rarely made explicit. Many of the practices and rules, and most of the curriculum, are taken for granted, as if their purpose needed no spelling out. This means that schools might be arcane, but are seen to have clear significance in the eyes of parents. For parents the school gives their own children a 'better chance than what we had'.[2] The school is a centre for respect and hope, as well as suspicion. It is an insurance policy against failure:

'My son thinks to be a footballer, but failing that he's very good at maths. He'd like to be an accountant, he'd like to go into a bank or something with computers — maths for him is very important.'

For parents schools fulfil a very definite function. Their very individuality of appearance, and completeness as institutions marks out their singularity in the scheme of things, as if whatever goes on inside them could not be carried out anywhere else. The whole point of school for the community is that it gives children the chance to leave with better qualifications:

'I just hope that it gives him a better chance in life; you know if he does well in school then they'll think, you know, he gets a better chance sort of afterwards when he *leaves* school.'

This is a traditional view. It suggests that the school provides children with the skills that they need for future employment. The employers in any community are assumed to demand the most traditional of skills, like maths and English. It is not surprising, therefore, that to parents the most significant subjects are the 'three Rs'.

Parents hold a traditional view of the curriculum, and of the methods of teaching and learning. Quite a number express bewilderment with modern styles of learning, through projects and individual working, rather than 'actual work . . . reading and writing'. These views, like the views of the whole community, are formed and coloured by the memories of their own experience. They tend to remember the most formal aspects of school, being taught in class, and being disciplined. This is one reason why so many parents feel that standards of discipline are falling. They partly wish that the school could do more to help them in their parental responsibility, but they also like the security of authority that they remember coming so easily from teachers:

'To be truthful, I don't think there's enough . . . punishment in schools. I'm a bit soft and I know they're my responsibility to bring the kids up, but I used to think when they go to school they'd be strict . . . I think they should be more stricter in school than they are.'

When schools are associated with the delivery of a moral code as well as a curriculum, their place in the consciousness of parents will be even stronger. The school is seen as having the power to

17

tell children about the difference between right and wrong. This makes the school powerful as well as mysterious. It is an experience shared between parents and children, even if it is not analysed or discussed. Every report that children make is tested against their parents' remembered and observed experience. As children are sensitive to their parents' response, their own attitudes to schools are to some extent influenced by their parents' memories.

Part of the mythology that surrounds school derives from the realization that teachers have an expertise beyond their communities. They know complex subjects like mathematics. They have a professional language about matters such as assessment that is all their own. Parents know that they could not fulfil the teacher's role. At the same time they do not think that teachers can do theirs. The expertise of teachers and the respect for them is embedded firmly in the school, which underlies the fact that the school is seen as an almost separate world.

The separation of the school from its surrounding community, symbolized by the closed nature of the activities that go on, and which no amount of trying to involve parents can really overcome,[3] suggests a type of schizophrenia for those involved with them. The private and public worlds of school overlap for parents and teachers as well as children. Long before they go to school children will have received distinct messages about schools, from their friends and siblings as well as their parents. Even when they visited the schools before going to them, they were presented with things to do, with activities rather than explanation. Children will have had to make sense of the world of the school in their own way. Their preliminary vision of school will be based on mythologies and rumour.

When schools try to explain their values and aims, their organization of the curriculum and their expectations, they do so primarily to parents. It is the parents who transmit these values to their children, charged as they are by the memory of their own experience. Sometimes there can be a conflict between parents' and teachers' attitudes to the school, given parents' suspicion of new teaching methods or less stringent habits of discipline. Even when parents are involved in the school, in helping children read, or helping children learn to cook pastry, they have a limited part to play. But they clearly transmit their hopes, indeed their concern, that their children do well:

'My parents want me to do well. My mum is pleased with how I'm getting on.' (girl, secondary)

Children are aware of their parents' interest in them individually and in the schools more generally, even if it is a subject that is not often discussed. They are aware of their parents' general fears:

'They were a bit worried . . . because it had a bad reputation.'
(boy, secondary)

Just as children pass a message to each other, about schools as well as teachers, so parents have a collective sense of schools' reputations, for their results as well as their ethos. They know which schools are 'rough' and which are 'good'. They make it clear when their children do not go to a school of their first choice:

'They wanted me to go to a good school like _____ or somewhere like that but the Head said I wouldn't be clever enough to pass the exams so I didn't get the chance. They were quite cross.' (girl, secondary)

Children know when their parents approve of the school, when they feel welcomed and involved and when they take an interest. They also know when they are critical. There can be clear disagreements in matters of teaching:

'My sister often comes home and says, "That's pathetic, the way they teach us to do that when there's an easier way like my dad can teach us." My dad often has to take her aside and explain it, and it's often a shorter way; it's much easier.' (girl, primary)

For many parents the work of the school is kept at a distance, not out of lack of interest but because it seems to be difficult or different:

'She came home with maths the other night and even my husband was completely dumbfounded. A certain amount of her work we can follow what they're doing, but some of the maths seems such a complicated way to get into what to us is simple adding and subtracting.'

Many parents feel that any help would be either confusing or interpreted as interference. The picture that they receive of what goes on in the classroom is often a confused one; for children are not inclined to give explanations of what they are doing in the separate world of the school. The common response to enquiries about what takes place in the school day is something along the lines of 'nothing'. When parents do hear more it tends to be something exceptional: an incident like bullying or a particularly difficult task. It is rare for children to know *exactly* what it is their parents expect:

> 'I draw pictures. That's what my mum wants me to do. I'll do that at the comp. My dad wants me to play snooker.'   (boy, primary)

The views of parents are both peculiar to their own children and a reflection on general attitudes. The community as a whole will pass on opinions about the decline of standards and the quality of different schools. It will also reflect on the views of politicians, highlighted in newspapers when they are negative. A general feeling about a decline in standards, and the lack of professionalism in teachers if they go on strike, pervades the more detailed attitudes to schools. Just as personal memory plays a part in attitude, so does the national obsession with blame. This colours the reputation of schools but does not give any precise picture of what they are like.

But if newspapers foster particular attitudes towards schools, there is another source of information that presents a series of stark images. Children in primary schools will be influenced in their perception of what it will be like at secondary level by the stories presented on television:

> 'Well, I am a bit scared because there will be lots of big children and they might boss you about a bit, and I've seen on TV lots of people in alley-ways stopping you from getting past or something like that. I think there'll be plenty of activities at the comp. because in films they have netball, and rugby and cricket.'   (girl, primary)

The picture of schools presented in series like *Grange Hill* is as potent as it may be inaccurate. Images, as in the school stories in comics, might be absurd and yet perpetuate a point of view.

Children look for information from any source, and some of the most potent sources are those which do not have designs on them. Whilst not being manipulated into a point of view, children absorb distinct impressions of the schools they will go to from the images they see, the majority of them being of secondary schools:

> 'In some programmes on TV about comps. they've got desks and some have got tables, so if they've got desks in the comp. it'll be all right.'   (girl, primary)

Naturally the children will look with particular attention at the scenes that connect directly to their own experience, as well as absorbing the more general attitudes. But it is in the connection of the two that the greatest influence lies. The reality becomes covered by a patina of exaggeration, glimpses of bullying or unfairness, of passion and misunderstanding that make a drama out of the everyday:

> 'I watch *Grange Hill* but I don't take very much notice of it. It's not real. Some of them are like real teachers but they're acting like real teachers. It's not really the same as school really. They're really only acting. Did you see the one where she got her hair cut off? I don't think this can really happen in comps. I don't believe most of it will come true.'   (boy, primary)

The information that children gather from a variety of overheard sources, from friends and from television, influences their attitudes to school in a subtle way. It is because the information is stereotyped and imaginative rather than analytic and descriptive that it carries influence. Primary school children, after years of experience of school life, still maintain clear stereotypes about secondary schools, as if there were two distinct pictures of the school experience rather than one. After the initiations into school life, through a mixture of experiences — play groups, play schools, nursery schools and nursery classes — children become accustomed to many of the essentials of institutional life. They adapt to various groups, to the organization of classes, to clear instructions and implicit rules. They understand the hierarchies of command. And yet, towards the end of their time in primary school, children build up a collective image of the secondary school that makes it seem like a wholly new experience.

Some of the mythologies about life in secondary school are

universal.[4] In all parts of the country children are told that part of the initiation ceremony consists of having their heads 'flushed down the loo'. Whether the experience is limited to birthdays or not, at some point all children meet the rumour:

> 'I wasn't really sure about it because I kept hearing tales about it, but on your birthday you get your head flushed down the loo and things like that.'
> (girl, secondary)

> 'I was afraid of being bullied and all the stories you heard in primary school about this school . . . like when it's your birthday people bunk you and take you to the toilets and flush your head down the loo.'
> (boy, secondary)

This symbolic rite of passage is part of the mythology that is passed from child to child; half believed in a mixture of fear and dismissal, taken as true and untrue at the same time.[5] Many of the rumours that children hear achieve a status similar to the stories told them flippantly and facetiously by adults when they are young. Are they to trust the person who says that babies are brought by storks? Are they to believe their friends' explanations of natural phenomena? They enjoy both hearing the stories and treating them as nothing more than stories. There is excitement in the telling and the receiving. It is as if there were an almost agreed network of ideas without source, of innuendo as effective as overheard remarks that have no designs on them.

The universality of the rumours about bullying says something about the way the children initiate each other into new circumstances and about the nature of communication. The information the children pass on to each other is often symbolic. It is designed both to surprise and encapsulate a circumstance in a story. The rumours are significant in their outlines of bullying, of rituals and of centres of power. They are both general and particular, about rules and individual teachers. And they convey a stereotype about schools that is never completely subsumed in the ritual practices of every day.

The most common sources of information about schools are not teachers, in their endeavours to explain, nor parents in their hopes and expectations. They are the children's friends and siblings. The kind of information they convey is unconventional.

A single incident can seem like a common occurrence. The anecdote carries many messages. Against this kind of communication, the facts conveyed by parents are not completely powerful. There is a tension between anecdotes and analysis:

'My brother says they all go bullying first-years and things like that but my mother says it's not true.' (girl, primary)

What children hear from each other carries more weight because it is not observation but a personal experience:

'Well I don't know because they used to pick up my brother a lot and he used to come home with blood on his shirt because they used to stick pens in him, and I'm a bit frightened of them. Hm . . . teachers. You hear they are pretty hard and things like that. My brother tells me the teachers are grumpy.' (girl, primary)

When children tell their younger brothers or sisters about their experience they naturally single out specific incidents that have particularly left their mark. The stories they relate are sometimes personal experiences and sometimes general insights:

'Because on the way home from the comp. my sister says these people keep going after her and she runs and they catch her and they try to thump her.' (girl, primary)

'My sister says at dinner time you have to stand for twenty minutes to get your dinner.' (boy, primary)

It is natural for children to talk of outstanding incidents or marked curiosities, since these will stand out in their minds. This leads to the tendency to pass on an exaggerated picture of the school, of a succession of highlights. But whilst elder brothers and sisters might enjoy the exaggerations, and even celebrate the toughness of the secondary school, in telling the stories that they pass on they are concerned mostly with incidents outside the classroom, with the less formal part of the educational system. When children relate their versions of the secondary school they suggest a more brutal world, of bullying and pain. This picture of school is not just a deliberate initiation into a new phase:

'I'd heard stories in the primary school about bullies and that . . .'

but one which continues once the traumatic change is over:

> 'It's scary because of all the stories about "bundle alley" and big kids bullying you.' (boy, secondary)

And the message that children receive is conveyed through personal experience, with evidence that gives substance to the more general rumours:

> 'My sister says these people keep going after her and she runs and they catch her and try to thump her.' (girl, primary)

Brothers and sisters are an important source of information because they convey immediate experience and the latest news. The insights younger siblings acquire are informed. There is less deliberate initiation, false exaggerations of rumour, than the overflowing of personal experience. Children hear of particular teachers and of the general atmosphere, of whom to look out for and whom to avoid:

> 'There's pushing about. Everybody's pushing and shoving. My friend says Mr ____'s quite a nice teacher up there.' (girl, primary)

> 'There's two big bullies and I know they go to that school now. They might still bully us. I've heard that they are getting bullied too.'
> (boy, primary)

The information network is far more extensive with children in the same family. When they are asked where they acquire this knowledge about schools, children very rarely cite teachers or parents. The formal mechanisms of transfer are very slight compared to the network of anecdotes. No general rule has as much salience as a personal incident that can be verified:

> 'Sometimes they get beaten up by the fourth year. It's true, I've seen it before.' (boy, primary)

> 'My friend went up there last year, and the second day he was there he got smashed in. He didn't know why. Some boys just for the fun of it smashed him in.' (boy, primary)

The one control that teachers have in the face of all the stories is to try to distinguish between rumours and anedotes:

> 'Flush your head down the loo. Our teacher said not to believe in it. That it didn't happen to anyone so don't believe it.'
> (girl, secondary)

The period of transfer from primary to secondary school is not only significant because it is a major rite of passage in children's lives. It is important as one of the very rare occasions when teachers are involved in talking about the nature of education. Clearly teachers' major concern is for a smooth transition between one kind of institution and another. They will bring out the similarities rather than the differences. They will not talk at any length about the underlying purposes of the schools. But they are, even if only slightly, party to what is a major item of interest to children throughout their school lives. For children are always engaged in, and concerned with, the inner realities of schooling, the relationships that institutions create, the consequences of rules, and the social habits of crowds of people. When the period of transfer arrives the ethos of different schools is brought to the fore. But whereas teachers stress the ease of transfer, children are aware of the contrasts between types of school. For those who know any subject really well, differences and distinctions will be more apparent.

There are many levels of contrast between schools. Transferring from one school to another of the same type has its problems. There can be contrasts of size and relationships:

'In Germany we had a thousand in the school. It was like Coronation Street. We knew the teachers only to speak to. We really didn't know them well. Just by name. Here you sort of know them personally, what they're really like.' (boy, primary)

There can be contrasts in details of organization:

'I like this school better than the one in Scotland. It was all blue books and there was no lines on the paper and you had to use a pencil. You weren't allowed to use a pen.' (girl, primary)

And there are also contrasts in teaching methods:

'. . . and then I started again here and did in a different way to the way I learned in Cheshire and that's when I started to get it all wrong.' (boy, primary)

Transfer makes children emphatically aware of what schools are like. In terms of their experience what matters most are the social aspects; what takes place between lessons. Their comments about the reputation of schools highlights their main concern.

25

When children describe what they think secondary schools are like, they convey a sense of fear. This is not just because of the rumours that abound. In fact children are themselves suspicious of what they are told:

'Michael, a boy who used to be here told me. I think it might be just to frighten me.' (boy, primary)

'He told me mostly lies . . . if you were naughty you'd get the cane, and all that rubbish . . .' (girl, secondary)

The sense of fear is fostered because they hear about everyday events, moving along corridors, constantly herded with other children. A major part of secondary school life is spent moving from place to place, waiting for doors to open, waiting for the bell. In this context the opportunities for subtle bullying are great. Such schools are then associated with being insecure. Whilst children are dismissive of some of the unreliable things they are told, and realize that there is a fascination in rumours as there is in story, the potency of the imagery remains. Rumours give a picture of life in a school which is strangely revealing.

The difference between 'official' descriptions of schooling and children's own shared experience is partly a matter of tone, and partly a matter of interpretation. The contrast lies between generalized outcomes and intimate experience. Even for children there is a contrast between their parents' and teachers' attitudes to school and their own. For children there is no escape. However critical adults may be they remain outsiders. Rumours have that special potency because they bind children together in their own personal experience. But children also accept the adult version of what schools really consist of, in parallel with their own. Just as the languages used to describe school are different from each other, so children come to think of schools as separate worlds. Schools are part of their own inner lives, but children live their lives rather differently there. The contrasts between life at home and life at school lie partly in the sense of discipline:

'If I was at home I'd miss the breaks and chats and being told off. When your mum and dad tell you off you tend to shout back at them. But you can't shout at the teacher. You'd get yourself a bad reputation. If your mum and dad give you reasons you don't take any notice. It keeps you good mannered and it's discipline and it's enjoyable. I like that.'   (girl, primary)

There are many cases when children do not like the worlds of school and home to overlap, and can be embarrassed by the presence of parents or teachers in each other's worlds. But they see both worlds as having distinct virtues. School, too, can be a relief:

> 'Well, I like a man and a lady teacher but I prefer a man. Mainly the men keep on saying that the women nag all the time. My mum nags all the time. I prefer me dad. Ladies nag at home but not at school. My mum nags day and night. It gets on my nerves. The only time my mum shuts up nagging is when "60 Minutes" comes on the telly.'
>   (boy, primary)

Sometimes the formality and anonymity of school can be a contrast to the more rugged experiences of life at home and in peer groups. But the two are distinct in children's minds, and they often keep the two almost secret from each other. This can be for pragmatic reasons.

> 'The main thing that worries me is if my mum's sick or me dad'll go beserk because one night I did something and got into quite a bit of a situation. You can't tell people what you've got inside you because you don't want them to know the things you don't want them to know. They could think badly of you. If you talked to teachers about it they might tell your parents.'   (boy, primary)

Although there are many occasions when the worlds of home and school overlap, the two remain essentially distinct. Sometimes the distinction is retained by their reluctance to relate what happens in one circumstance, when in the other. Sometimes they are so exclusive about the difference it is like an embarrassment for them to have the two drawn together. But both home and school make up the complete world of children. Their wishes and their faults are clear in contrast. Children can clearly long, when in one place, to be in the other, for each has is own kind of relief. At home as well as school children go through tracts of boredom:

> 'I like school because if you stay at home all day you do nothing and it's a bit boring.'   (girl, primary)

27

Whilst many hours can be spent watching television at home, which is sometimes seen as a relief after the demands of school, it can become boring in excess.[6] Schools, after all, provide children with a social meeting place, and with structured activities. There children are told what to do, and do not have to entertain themselves:

> 'You get bored at home and you've got nothing to do. It's nice here; you get lots to do and friends to play with.'   (girl, primary)

For many children going back to school after holidays is a relief from boredom. Even weekends seem difficult to cope with without the routines of school. The children readily admit to being bored at home; so that schools begin to play a distinct part even in their social life:

> 'It's better than being stuck in the house watching telly all day. On Saturdays I sometimes get so bored so I learn my tables.'
>
> (boy, primary)

> 'I just get bored at home. I find at the weekend it's all right but on Sunday I get really bored.'   (girl, secondary)

Children can, of course, be as bored at school as they are at home. Their propensity to boredom is never that far away. They can be bored by routine lessons as well as the routines of home, by waiting for things to happen to them as well as by the boredom of constantly being entertained. Whether boredom is a symptom of a state of mind or a necessary part in the development of the mind remains an unexplored question. But it is clear that many children are not constantly absorbed in the excitement of everyday events, and that they do not know where to turn for stimulation. It is for this reason that television can be at once so popular and so despised. It mitigates boredom and at the same time encourages it. But the boredom which is having nothing to do is linked peculiarly with home. At school children become accustomed to being told. They do not have to create pleasures or make things happen. If they find school tedious it is through repetition of the same material, or waiting for the next instruction. It is the sheer number of events that makes schools demanding. It is the threat of bullying that makes them frightening. The boredoms of home can then appear the more attractive.

Schools impose a structure to the day. This can feel like an imposition but can also be an easy framework to exist in. Being at home then becomes a contrast which can be a responsibility as well as a relief. Home becomes associated with release; and the end of the school day is anticipated with pleasure:

> 'Home time 'cos you can do more things when you get home. You can play and that. Watch the telly.'   (girl, primary)

When going home is a relief after all the demands made by school, homework becomes something particularly intrusive:

> 'I got home. I've been doing lots and lots of work at school and as soon as I get home — more work. I think school's long enough as it is, without having to have homework as well.'   (boy, secondary)

Children do not resent the idea of homework in itself, provided that teachers spend time marking it. They dislike it, mildly. But they do resent homework when it intrudes substantially on their association of home and relaxation. For at home they wish to enter into the communal distractions of the living-room:

> 'If I do it up in my bedroom, it's OK but if I do it downstairs it's not. But I don't really like being up in my bedroom — alone — no radio or TV — on, all on your own.'   (girl, secondary)

Children's reflections on their lives at home reveal something important about the place of school in their lives. Their association of home with personal liberty and luxury, with boredom and responsibility, shows how clearly marked in their minds is the school as an institution, as a system of management. Life at school and life at home are seen as different, so that the unique place schools have in the lives of their communities is built into their minds at an early stage. After school children go through a different kind of routine:

> 'I go home, watch TV, have my tea and then go out to my friends.'
>   (boy, secondary)

The pace is different, and the contrast in style and attitudes quite clear. In one place they organize themselves often in a desultory way. In the other, organization is thrust upon them. Just as much time might be wasted, but in a different way.

The reputation of schools is fixed firmly in the minds of those who will enter them long before they do so. Schools appear as the essence of institutional organization. They seem to be like factories in their collective endeavour, except that they have no obvious product. Those in them become part of a process. The imagery that children reveal to each other in anecdotes shows that many of the most significant events are a by-product of institutional crowding. Both the good moments of school and the terrible half-hours are a result of the particular socialization school presents.

NOTES AND REFERENCES

1. White, R. with Brockington, D. *Tales out of School: Consumers' Views of British Education*. London: Routledge and Kegan Paul, 1983.
2. Cullingford, C. *Parents, Teachers and Schools*. London: Robert Royce, 1985, esp. pp. 131–51.
3. See the experiences cited by Thomas, G. 'The teacher and others in the classroom,' in Cullingford, C. *The Primary Teacher*. London: Cassell, 1989, pp. 56–74.
4. Measor, L. and Woods, P. *Changing Schools: Pupils Perspectives on Transfer to a Comprehensive*. Milton Keynes: Open University Press, 1984.
5. Cf. Pears, D. *Motivated Irrationality*. Oxford: Oxford University Press, 1984.
6. Cullingford, C. *Children and Television*. Aldershot: Gower, 1984.

CHAPTER 4

The Atmosphere of Schools

'It's nicest in your classroom when there is no one else there.'

(girl, primary)

From warning signs and special road crossings to playing fields or playgrounds, schools have a distinctive physical presence. The way that they are built, old or new, makes statements about what they stand for and how they go about achieving their aims. The whole community, or society, is expressed in the state of the walls, or the temporary classrooms, in the treatment of the windows and the halls. A visitor to a town or suburb will automatically judge it by its appearance, knowing how much she is affected by it. A visitor to a school will be just as affected by its appearance, even if there is a tendency to assume that all schools look rather alike.

We readily make judgements about the beauty or ugliness of different towns and cities. And we know that appearances have their effects. Architects are aware that their buildings affect those who will live in them, that differences of space and colour can have definite psychological influences. But such analyses of the effects of buildings are rarely applied to schools. The architecture of schools is more often discussed in terms of the uses that are made of different kinds of space than in terms of the effects of space.[1] Perhaps we take too much for granted, assuming that what schools need is the product of utilitarian questions — so much space for so little money, as with factories and warehouses — rather than the result of aesthetic ones. Perhaps we take for granted that all schools will be covered with displays of children's work, disguising the lack of quality in the material used to build them.

Children are, however, profoundly affected by atmospheres. They respond immediately to certain kinds of weather, like the wind. They are also sensitive to physical appearance, having favourite places, and places they would prefer to avoid. They are also aware of the differences in the appearance of classrooms and the use made of work displays.[2] They like decorations that are

31

aesthetically pleasing: a desire not often met.

The problem for children is that the appearance of many schools is based on well-intentioned routine. Schools are visually crowded spaces. There are few surfaces of walls that are not covered up, sometimes in a carefully staged display, more often in a jumble of children's work. And for nearly all the time these work displays are no more than decorations. They are neither looked at closely, nor remembered. Indeed children are unaware of what is up on the walls, beyond knowing where their own work is. The effect of wall displays is, then, a purely decorative one; giving a familiar covering to walls that might otherwise look bleak or badly maintained. But it is an effect, none the less.

Schools have three distinct types of space to deal with: the hall, the classroom and the corridor. Each is a type of room that is not found anywhere else in the same way. The hall can be used for assemblies, television presentations, lunch or gym. It is constantly being cleared up for different functions. The classroom is, even in open-plan schools, a distinct space, closed in by displays, sets of books and materials and filled with tables or desks and chairs. And the corridors are places where children do not only pass, but wait. They are often the only places where children can, ostensibly, work by themselves.

In all these areas children spend a significant proportion of their time waiting for something to happen. They wait for the next question or the next instruction. They wait before they begin their work, or before they begin to tidy up. It is difficult to calculate the exact amount of time that is spent between bouts of activity. In some schools where classes were followed for a day, it was calculated that more than three-quarters of children's time was spent waiting for something to happen.[3] The notion of 'time on task' gives some indication of the difference between activity and waiting time.[4] But 'time on task' only measures ostensible work, marking out the visible activity of reading and writing. It does not calculate the difference between copying out or regurgitating material and exploring a new concept. Even at that level the time that children spend absorbed in work is worryingly low.[5]

The most ideal system could not demand complete concentration all the time. It is not expected in adult working life, and even in a laboratory the labour of steady intellectual work cannot be kept up hour after hour. But the fact that children have many distractions from work within their classrooms is a significant part of their school experience. This 'waiting' within the classroom is in addition to waiting in queues, to enter a room or the hall for lunch. There are many moments both within and outside the classroom when children are talking, or observing, or simply doing nothing. How else is it possible for so many children to produce so little after a morning at their desk? The labour that has gone into the half a side of A4 — creative writing, perhaps — is not the labour of fierce perfectionism to make sure that the words are just the ones they want to use. The work is far more likely to be a product of doing a minimum to keep the teacher happy, or at least a sign that something is being done.

We all know the difference between the kind of work that can make the brain ache and the routines of fulfilling undemanding duties. Children early become aware of the distinction between something that absorbs them completely, and more mechanical routines. Schools unwittingly encourage this distinction. Ordering a large number of people into small spaces at a certain time, or taking the register and dinner money, or tidying up or distributing materials, and controlling the movement from one place to another, makes a necessity of quiet, routine, waiting. Such attention to details of order are specifically seen, in the Education Reform Act, as having nothing to do with the time spent on the curriculum. And yet schools can only function if there is some measure of order, and that means the rituals of waiting.

But most waiting takes place in the classroom, before a task, during a task and after a task. It can entail talking to a neighbour, walking round the class, standing at a desk, or just sitting and looking. This all takes place in a distinct environment in which children spend more than half their lives. The general appearance of the classroom in terms of its facilities and the care taken with the wall displays makes a distinct impression on the children. It symbolizes the attention that is paid to the quality of learning. Just as children expect a clear sense of order, so they hope for a comfortable environment. The variations between classrooms are not that great, given the paucity of the resources available. But to children they are significant. At their own homes they try to make their own rooms comfortable to be in, with materials they can associate with pleasure. They speak of those places they enjoy being in and the places they find gloomy. Children notice neglect and ugliness within the school, just as they clearly observe the quality of the environment in which they live.[6]

Children in primary school remark on the effort, or lack of it, that goes into making their surroundings pleasant. They like a feeling of 'warmth' in a room, and like carpet, even if it is inevitably restricted to just one corner of a room. They like rooms to be 'bright and cheerful'. They appreciate having their own work displayed — 'for passers-by to see'. And they like to have the walls covered in displays because there is no other decoration so readily available. 'If the walls were bare it would be pretty boring.' Drab corridors and dull classrooms become symbolic of indifference and lack of interest.

Children feel strongly and consistently about the need for privacy and personal space, for the cheerfulness of familiar surroundings and the security of the home base where they know where everything can be found. Much of this sense of place is associated with the primary school and a particular way of working. But children are then transferred to a quite different environment, not only bigger and full of mobility but looking different and not providing the same sense of an aesthetic devoted to the children's own work. To children, the secondary school seems to be the 'real', the 'more important' world and less secure and comfortable. They therefore need very quickly to adapt to their new surroundings. Some of them look back on the classrooms of primary schools and note how changed are the circumstances of secondary schools with their variety of environments.

'In the primary I was always in the same class all the time, looking at the same old walls and the old pictures on the walls and that, and this time if I go to the French class I've got French things on the walls, and in the English class, English things.'　　(boy, secondary)

In both kinds of school the same concerns remain; the need for privacy and security and the desire for cheerful surroundings. For most children their favourite places in a school are those which provide them with relief from the hurly-burly of school life, either within the classroom, or somewhere else:

> 'There's a dull corner where there's strong currents and swirling winds . . . those who are lonely or don't have friends or aren't liked by someone or are just in that mood, they just sort of stand there with their friends chatting quietly.' (girl, secondary)

Sometimes the classrooms themselves offer the quietness, when there are not too many people in them, for even places supposed to be quiet can be overcome by people 'chattering all the time'. 'There's a quiet corner that isn't really quiet.'

For many children schools can be fearful places, but they also contain moments of cheerfulness or warmth, friendships and a secure sense of purpose. Children derive pleasure from those moments when they are engaged in an activity that they enjoy and share with others. They like the times when they are free of the hassles of new and different demands, of teachers, exams and other pupils. Just as they fear undertaking tasks that they do not understand, so children consciously enjoy the moments of such absorption that work, whether reading or another activity, becomes its own reward and security. For primary school children the symbol of such security is the comfortable classroom with which they are familiar. They see it as a haven which contrasts with other activities, even the demands made by the teachers in the classroom:

> 'It's good being in the same classroom all day because you know where you are going and you get to know your classroom so you feel comfortable there.' (girl, primary)

The classroom can be as familiar as home, and appreciated for its security. Children often refer to the fact that they are 'used to it':

> 'It's big and quite warm. I like being in the classroom 'cos I can sit on a table on my own and nobody's there.' (girl, primary)

> 'I just like our class. It's a nice place. It's a bit more safe than being outside. Plus it's much more warmer. It's a good place to work and it's more comfortable. Normally we can laugh.' (boy, primary)

But it is not only primary school children who appreciate the security of the home base, with a familiar routine and familiar surroundings. Secondary children look back on the primary school with a certain nostalgia for a different way of working, for the security and peace that the classroom can give. They do not long to revert to that style of organization but they do continue to associate security with the primary base, where they did not have to move around from classroom to classroom:

> 'I would like a little room that anybody can use, but one class at a time, not one person from every class because the library's noisy because classes keep going through there and people keep talking to get through there. . . .' (girl, secondary)

> 'It's best in your classroom when there's no one in there. It's really quiet then.' (girl, secondary)

The sense of place with which children associated the security of being undisturbed is not only felt in general terms of a particular classroom with its own atmosphere and familiarity. They also like their own particular part in the classroom; their seat, their view and the table at which they can congregate with their friends. Their own position within the room may be due to an arbitrary decision of the teacher but it is not arbitrary to the children, who can quickly foster a particular liking for a particular place. Sometimes this can depend on who else is sitting with them, but sometimes it derives from a significant feature, like the view:

> 'I like being in the same classroom all day . . . I prefer to sit next to a window all the time so that I can look out.' (girl, primary)

> 'I sit by the window . . . I choosed it there . . . my partner wanted to sit there so I sit with him.' (boy, primary)

One of the fears of the transfer to the secondary school is the loss of the security of a home base:

> 'I like to work in my room as everybody is around you and you can hear people walking about and children talking and everything . . . I won't like moving from classroom to classroom very much because I don't like moving about much.' (boy, primary)

The classroom is not the only place singled out for peace and quiet. There are many other places in primary and secondary schools that provide security and privacy. Such places can be found in corridors, in the peace of the library, or outside the headteacher's room:

'The library . . . somewhere in a corner where it would be quiet . . . that's one of the places. The other place is in the office area; it's nice and quiet there. There are some library books there if you want to come in and read so if you're bored you can come in and read.'

(girl, primary)

'The library because it was always kind of quiet; and in the playground everybody was shouting.'
(boy, primary)

'There was a little place near the headmaster's office. It has little poem books and you could go and sit there between breaks.'

(girl, primary)

Many children suggest that they need some quiet place where they will be undisturbed. They also imply that this is not easy to find. The classroom is obviously one place where there is a break from the hurly-burly of the normal school routine, but it is not the only place, nor always the best one. Every child appreciates the possibilities of finding some quiet and private place:

'I like the block where we go and watch television. There's nobody running around or working down there and we just sit down and watch the telly. It's quiet and I like doing that sometimes.'

(boy, primary)

'I like to be in somewhere where people can't see me. If I have to sharpen my pencil, I usually go into the toilets to wash my hands as well, so I can get a bit of time away from the work; just a break. I'll have to think a new thing up at the comp. to get away.'

(girl, primary)

Children fear that there are few places in the secondary school for them to enjoy those moments of solitude they all crave. The need for privacy remains important to them, especially in contrast to the crowdedness of corridors. They do not want to be constantly disturbed and they all express the desire for finding privacy, even if the only place in which to be by onself is the lavatory:

'To the girls' loos for privacy . . . I don't know anywhere else.'
(boy, secondary)

37

'To the toilets . . . but on the other hand I might not because the teachers lock all the doors at play time, so all I do is go into a corner.'

(girl, secondary)

In the secondary school, as in the primary, the library serves an emotional as well as an intellectual purpose:

'The library . . . it's nice and quiet and I go to the place where my set of books are and there's usually nobody there, because nobody's really interested in what I'm interested in.' (boy, secondary)

The library, however, is not always the first place that comes to mind when children talk about quiet moments in the secondary school:

'You'd go to the loos for privacy, because this all gets locked up at dinner time so you can't really find anywhere to go.'

(girl, secondary)

'The bicycle sheds. It's quiet there.' (boy, secondary)

It is easy to forget that one of the facts of school experience is that the day is largely spent not only in the company of other people but in collective activities. Home is the main place for privacy; and yet all children talk about the desire for more undisturbed moments, as well as their pleasure in those times when they can go somewhere quiet. The classroom is the obvious centre for quiet moments in the primary school. The quiet corner is more difficult to find in the comprehensive school.

Primary schools seem to the children altogether safer places: there are clear relationships with teachers and with their friends. The classroom is symbolic of that sense of permanence, a feeling that secondary school children clearly do not feel is appropriate for their age. Nevertheless many children hope that, despite what they know about secondary schools, there will be some place in which they will find some peace and quiet:

'I like being in the fields . . . I love that in the summer by myself, so I think there'll be somewhere like that at secondary school.'

(girl, primary)

It has already been pointed out how unlike any other institutions schools are, and how important a formative influence for year

38

after impressionable year. The distinctiveness of schools is a generalizable phenomenon deeper than all the differences between them. We know how differently schools perform and how varied is the ethos of different schools.[7] And yet schooling is a distinct common experience, recognizable to all who have been to school. The ways in which people are organized, the imposition of rules and the patterns of friendship and bullying are all as distinct as the nature and appearance of classrooms and corridors. But just as there are aspects of the experience of school which are common to all, so, at a different level, it is equally true to say that there are two different stereotypes of school, the primary and the secondary. The ways in which the two types of school present themselves have differences as well as similarities. Their outward appearance symbolizes differences in ethos, in the relationships between teachers, parents and children. In primary schools the sense of security, the closeness of the home and the relationship with one teacher makes a sense of wholeness both in the curriculum and in the appearance of classrooms. In secondary schools many aspects of holistic learning are replaced by more specialized relationships and a more specialized curriculum.

One of the most difficult passages of childhood is the transfer from primary to secondary school. In the minds of parents as well as their children the change from one type of school to another is a symbolic movement from the innocence of childhood to the troubles of adolescence. For the children the change from the relative safety and security of the primary school to the harsher demands of the comprehensive is one to which they do not look forward.[8] Such a contrast between one set of attitudes and circumstances and another is more than symbolic. There is no question about some of the differences between primary and secondary schools. At one level such contrasts are obvious; in terms of size and in terms of organization. The experiences that children have are quite different, from staying in one base to moving from classroom to classroom, from a relationship developed over time with one teacher to the response to a succession of different teachers in different places. But the contrasts also reveal some of the underlying unities that hold good in children's attitudes to both types of establishment. These include their perception of teachers and the curriculum, the atmosphere and the environment and the sense of discipline. At one level it is as if there were two different traditions of schooling. At another children make something coherently their own out of both.

In the difficult passage from one type of school to another children learn to adapt and to make sense of the connections between one experience and the other, partly because of their consistent views of the purpose of education. The experiences nevertheless are very different, and they are aware of this difference both before and after the transfer. Most of the differences between primary and secondary schools are obvious. Secondary schools are always far bigger, with bigger people, larger masses of people in corridors and with more of a sense of scrambling from one place to another. Given that children entering secondary school find themselves amongst the smallest, and least able to protect themselves, it is not surprising that the size of the school is often mentioned in anticipation by primary school children:

'It will be difficult to find our way around because it is so big.'
(boy, primary)

'I didn't think anybody would want to know me.'　(girl, primary)

The one clear image that primary children have is the contrast between themselves and the masses they will be joining, in larger and more impersonal spaces:

'It's going to be a lot bigger which means you can go round and get lost.'　(girl, primary)

The sense of awe at the size and the sense of being lost amongst so many people permeates the reactions of primary school children. But they soon become accustomed to it, and although *all* secondary children remember being scared when they first arrived, they point out how quickly they fit in:

'It was a bit scary at first, but I've got the hang of it.'
(girl, secondary)

'It's bigger . . . I was scared at first.'　(boy, secondary)

40

Nevertheless, the first day or two strike children as being traumatic:

> 'It was terrible at first — you couldn't find your way around. There was other things, like . . . worried about the places and trying to find out where you are and all that.' (boy, secondary)

The terms that keep appearing are 'scary', 'horrible', 'frightening' and 'nervewracking', referring both to the effect of the place and to their own response to it:

> 'At first you're petrified. You don't know what's going to happen or anything . . . the moving about, things like that.' (girl, secondary)

The sense of size in the secondary school is conveyed not just in physical appearance but in the organization which makes the probability of feeling lost so much greater.

The second obvious contrast in the minds of the children is the need to move from lesson to lesson as opposed to having a particular place which they feel is their own. For primary school children, secondary schools are characterized by short lessons, a rush from classroom to classroom, and from teacher to teacher, with a certain amount of bullying on the way. For secondary school children the movement from class to class, and the shortness of the lessons is no longer 'frightening' but an opportunity for pleasurable mischief. Many of them feel that secondary schools are more lenient in terms of teacher control since they are out of sight of those who are supposed to maintain discipline for a considerable amount of time. It is certainly true that the conditions in secondary schools make it harder to impose a sense of order and control. But from the distance of the primary school the movement between classrooms has a number of significant factors:

> 'You don't hardly read really at the comp.; you go into different classes.' (boy, primary)

> 'It's going to be much harder work. Very big. I'll get lost. I'll probably end up in the wrong class. It will be a bit scary at first.' (girl, primary)

> '. . . different kinds of lessons 'coz we need exams so they'll know how good you are, the teachers . . . different people, different teachers.' (boy, primary)

41

'The comp's more important ... bigger. You switch classrooms — everybody's pushing and shoving.'   (girl, primary)

For primary children different teachers and different classes imply not only being afraid, or being bullied, but higher standards and more work. Secondary children remember their first bewilderment but forget their expectation of higher standards. They are aware of the variety of experiences the new system gives them; not uniformly higher standards, but differences in style between teachers:

'... now I'm used to it ... I got lost once, didn't know what it was like. In between every lesson you know what you're doing next, and you go to different teachers all the time.'   (boy, secondary)

'We have to move around and go to different teachers, you learn lots of different things ... I suppose it's fun in a way, find out your timetable, where you're going and seeing a new teacher.'
(girl, secondary)

'Well, they [the lessons] are shorter, you had time to finish your work there and you haven't got it here ... it's more varied apart from moving around, and you have more lessons.'   (girl, secondary)

'It's different because the teachers do one thing, then you have to change classrooms for the other teacher to teach you the other things.'
(boy, secondary)

Even if there were not so many experiences of different teaching methods, the secondary school pupils would nevertheless associate their school with greater specialisms and with better equipment. How else can they explain to themselves the constant shifting from place to place?

Children in secondary schools not only adapt to different expectations and attitudes expressed by a variety of teachers, but to different teaching spaces. The environment of secondary schools is dictated by specialist rooms — for art, for science, for craft, design and technology — in addition to the relatively empty spaces left for the humanities. In each type of room there are different kinds of workbench as well as equipment, so that children grow accustomed to the crucial differences between subjects. Learning is no longer an exploration by a group but is presented as a variety of environments, demanding not only different forms of communication but different styles of working. This contrast between rooms both dictates and highlights the need for movement.

Few aspects of secondary school strike children in their first year after transfer more forcibly than the constant moving around. Some children feel that the most sensible reform of secondary schools would be the provision of larger corridors, for they all agree that the movements from classroom to classroom are a constant 'rite of passage':

'You go from higher to lower [school] like a yo-yo.'

(boy, secondary)

'Getting pushed and shoved going to different lessons — I have got used to it, I suppose, but it's still not nice.'   (girl, secondary)

'I don't like all the going backwards and forwards, like this afternoon we have first lesson in the Upper School, then the second in the Lower School, and then back to the Upper School. I suppose I've got used to it.'   (girl, secondary)

'But stairs get overcrowded — pushing about — I get pushed about.'

(boy, secondary)

When children point out that it would be sensible to have larger corridors they are observing pragmatically how badly many schools are designed for the purposes to which they will be put. Clearly one of the fundamental briefs given to architects is concerned less with people than with saving money. This was a primary reason for the support of the idea of 'open-plan' schools. A potential educational principle was given weight by the possibility of spending less money on walls. Even primary schools have to transfer large numbers of pupils from one place to another. But in secondary schools such transfers are a fundamental principle that makes corridors such a significant feature in children's experience. The corridors, constantly overcrowded, often bleak, are opportunities for talking and bullying, but also for the informal pleasures of school. The constant moving about gives children a sense of escape:

'It gives you a break from teachers'; 'Not always stuck there all day.'

> 'I like the day all broken up with different teachers. It gives you a chance to eat bubble gum and things.' (girl, secondary)

Constant movement is accepted by children as an inevitable consequence of greater specialism and a greater demarcation of the curriculum. Children sense that secondary schools are more demanding because they are closer to the 'real' world of work, that primary schools are just a first stage of preparation for the harder demands of the secondary school:

> 'The work will be different because they'll do work more properly than in the primary school.' (boy, primary)

Moving from place to place seems justified because:

> 'You've got more things to learn.' (girl, primary)

All primary school children assume that the work in secondary school will be harder. This assumption derives from the fact that there are distinct subjects, and distinct places for separate subjects and separate teachers, each one a specialist. Primary schools are homogeneous by contrast, and therefore assumed by children to be poorly equipped both at the level of resource and in the demands made by teachers. The secondary school is anticipated as offering 'more exciting science' and making sure 'there'll be a lot more things you have to do'.

> 'You have a different tutor for everything. You can't get to know one. You're going to have to know about everything and there'll be a lot more subjects.' (girl, primary)

> 'You can go to science and then to English. It's like a timetable. You don't do it here because you don't know about it and you might get mixed up. You probably get used to it at the comp.' (boy, primary)

This impression is immediately confirmed by those who have entered secondary school.

The picture of the secondary school as a place of constant movement, of bustle and pushing and crowds attempting to find their way to specialist rooms, is an aspect of children's sense of its importance, as if the world of work will be like that. Against such a series of stops and starts primary schools appear far more settled, less adult, with a 'home' base and a sense of time to carry out work. The very fact that the primary school is perceived as settled makes children subsequently assume that the world of the primary school is both less intense and less significant. The primary school, like the secondary school, is seen as a stage in the development towards employment, each successive stage becoming more important:

> 'Primary school teaches you the basic things before you go on to more complicated things.'
> (girl, primary)

> 'The primary school sets you up for the secondary school.'
> (boy, primary)

> 'Well, from when I was a little one I've always wanted to go up to the next higher school. I want to go to college or university. It gets harder as you get older, doesn't it?'
> (girl, primary)

At the back of their minds primary school children realize why the transfer to a secondary school is so important:

> ''cos you learn more there. When you grow up you'll need a job.'
> (girl, primary)

> 'The comp's to learn things. You learn all the things. Then you have to have a test. You have to do science. It's for when you get a job.'
> (boy, primary)

Whatever the underlying necessity of transfer to the secondary school, and its greater importance, the actual experience nevertheless strikes children as difficult. There is a sense of bewilderment in being confronted by such a change of circumstances:

> 'You have to go to one classroom, then another classroom and there's different lessons and different teachers. You wear a uniform. I don't know why.'
> (girl, primary)

The bewilderment does not prevent all the children agreeing that such an experience is 'the real thing' and the primary school 'is not so important'. But they are aware of the contrasts in the environment and of the way in which the differences symbolize two different traditions of school. The secondary school lacks a

45

firm base; the primary school appears the more comfortable and pleasant.

NOTES AND REFERENCES

1. Bennett, N., Andreae, J., Hegarty, P. and Wade, B. *Open Plan Schools: Teaching, Curriculum: Design.* Windsor: NFER Publishing, 1980.
2. Cullingford, C. 'Wall displays: children's reactions.' *Education 3–13*, **6** (2), 12–14, 1978.
3. Research carried out by the author in different schools in the South Midlands, following particular classes through the experience of complete school days.
4. Bennett, N., Desforges, C., Cockburn, A. and Wilkinson, B. *The Quality of Pupil Learning Experiences.* London: Lawrence Erlbaum, 1984.
5. *Ibid.*
6. Cullingford, C. *Children and Society* (forthcoming).
7. Mortimore, P., Sammons, P., Stoll, L., Lewis, D. and Ecob, R. *School Matters: The Junior Years.* London: Open Books, 1988.
8. Measor, L. and Woods, P. *Changing Schools: Pupil Perspectives on Transfer to a Comprehensive.* Milton Keynes: Open University Press, 1984.

CHAPTER 5

The Personal Experience of School

'It's not as bad as I thought it was going to be. You don't usually get on in class . . . because they're always mucking about and you can't help having a good giggle about it.'　(girl, secondary)

Most institutions are public places which provide private experiences. Schools seem public to those in them, but are, in fact, fairly exclusive. Many of the private experiences are shared with others. For schools provide the chance to meet a large number of other children. They accumulate in small groups and large, within the classroom and outside. There are few chances for anyone to be alone. Instead, children spend their time exploring friendships, understanding relationships and sharing their learning with each other.[1] If there are a few occasions when children can be by themselves, there are many opportunities for discussion.[2] Children talk to each other in the classrooms and they discuss their ideas while sharing a task. In fact many of the issues that are most important to children are explored not by the class as a whole, or with teachers, but with each other. Their families, the meaning of life, their favourite programmes or interests, politics and their environments are all part of a fabric of conversation through which peer group attitudes are formed. Beneath a panoply of set tasks and a given curriculum lies a mass of exploration, through anecdote and analysis, personal observation and generalization of experience.

Those parts of the day that are spent in waiting are not given over just to day-dreaming or emptiness. They are also an important part of children's learning, of attitudes and relationships. It is through children's connections with each other that they form attitudes towards work, and towards the general ethos of the school.[3] Children learn from each other what they can get away with in terms of work and behaviour and pass on messages about each teacher's style. They then learn not only about their schools but about all those things which are of current debate and which are almost always ignored by the official curriculum of the school.

An important strand of a child's development is that initiation into the shared experiences of the group. The real culture of a school involves the playground as much as the classroom. What is called the 'hidden' curriculum consists not only of the implications that underlie the more formal curriculum, but the constant sharing of information that takes place all the time. Information may be delivered in lessons, but attitudes towards this information are passed on amongst the children themselves, through discussions and overheard remarks.

Even as a physical entity the school is a meeting place, an opportunity not just to learn but to meet friends. For many teachers this aspect of school is important.[4] Children need to learn how to relate to each other as well as to teachers; they need to learn the rituals of expected behaviour as well as the rules of enforced behaviour. Children themselves are aware of the importance of this. They know that their happiness in school depends not so much on the quality of lessons as on the way they can develop their relationships with other children. When they are unhappy enough to take their discontent home and talk about school the cause is, as often as not, the loss of a friendship, or bullying. Children spend much of their time in school subconsciously reflecting on how to get on with others, how to make a friendship or how to avoid being isolated or teased. They acknowledge that schools provide them with opportunities to meet others and to learn how to come to terms with them. School is a meeting place that forces children to adapt:

'If you didn't meet anybody else you wouldn't be socialized.'

(boy, primary)

A school's virtues derive from the pleasures of friendship; its terrors from loneliness and isolation.

Those who talk of the curriculum and of what should be 'delivered' by schools can speak in studied simplicities. Those who know schools and observe the way they operate recognize that what is learned by children is not just a matter of attention paid to information given by teachers. Even within the classroom there are many complex messages and children learn as much from each other as from the teacher. The school as a whole consists of a greater world than that of the classroom. Part of the school's complexity lies in the different levels of meaning between the ostensible curriculum and the 'hidden' curriculum. Part of it lies in the fact that the operation of moving from class to class, or to the assembly hall or to cloakrooms provides for a multitude of social interactions, even more difficult than those of the classroom. From a child's perspective the experience of school includes arrival, the activities of the playground, dinner time and all the many occasions on which she is not paying close attention to a look or to the voice of the teacher. Even within the classroom much of the time is spent moving around, waiting and changing places.

When children talk about the purpose of schooling they have as clear and single-minded an idea as those who have designs on the curriculum. But when it comes to their experience of school it is clear that many of the other activities of school have equal significance. Extra-curricular activities are as important for them as the routines of breaks and lunch. When children assess what school is like, they are as likely to point out that it gives the opportunity to meet other people and the chance to be with friends as they are to suggest the importance of lessons. At one level children formally acknowledge the importance of mathematics and English. But they also recognize that personal friendships dominate their experience.

The great advantage of school, for children, is that it is the great meeting place in which many activities can take place. Primary and secondary schools contrast in size, organization and ethos but both provide opportunities to meet other children, a facility given by no other institution in the same way or in the same numbers. Teachers talk about the importance of socialization as a central aspect of schooling: children are conscious of the chance to meet their friends as a matter of pleasure:

'It's quite nice. I don't mind working, either. You can meet your friends and you can do interesting things sometimes.'

(boy, primary)

School is, after all, the central place which gives opportunities for friendship:

'Primary school should be fun and it is. Well, the fun with being with your friends around you and in the lessons you can actually see them

49

around you. You're not locked away in a little cage sort of thing and you never come out. You have breaks and dinners. . . .'

(girl, primary)

It is because of this aspect of school that children look forward to returning after the vacations. Friends make school pleasurable. They alleviate the tedium, protect from potential unhappiness and provide the most memorable moments. Although children hope for steady and friendly relationships with teachers they do not confuse the types of relationship they would have with them and with their own peers. The one similarity is the way in which children experiment with both relationships, seeing how they can develop them and whether they can change the tone. It is almost as if they were deliberately exploring the possibilities of relationships, occasionally playing parts, often changing their feelings for others with great rapidity.[5] Friendship patterns, between individuals and groups, are constantly changing.

Within the almost experimental nature of changing relationships children can look at what is happening with a degree of detachment that can be surprising. They are aware of where they themselves stand in the hierarchy of academic achievement, and they know which girls and boys are most popular. They are honest about their own personal popularity, about which nearly all feel confident. They take for granted that having friends and being liked go together. But they also convey an honest assessment of the realities of their own circumstances. If they are *not* popular they know it: 'I'm not really popular. I get picked on.' And they do not seem to be particularly concerned. They do not mind not being liked by certain people, since this assessment is in the context of a general confidence in themselves.

Children's feelings about school, and about their work, depend as much on their success with other children as on their capacity to work. They feel that when they are with friends they are more successful. Those who like others are liked in their turn. Working in a supportive atmosphere is felt to be essential, and does not undermine their sense of competition or the differences in achievement. Being used to the support of friends means that the loss of familiar companions on going to a new school can be a worry:

'I didn't like it in the beginning because I didn't think anybody would want to know me. Then when ____ started to play with me I started to enjoy it.'

(girl, secondary)

Every school is a new challenge to children's ability to make friends. Given a large number of acquaintances they can change companions easily. Confronted by many strangers, all of whom *seem* to know others, making new relationships is more difficult. At first children cling to friends they had at previous schools or, failing that, to anyone with whom they struck up a relationship. But the friendships of the first few days are soon over. Gradually children learn enough about the context of all their peers to choose afresh, and begin a series of new experiments.

As children become older, friendship becomes more of a challenge. Friends are no longer part of the collecting of experience, being replaced rapidly one by one, but become more intense and complicated. But just as there are fewer changes of friends, and more intense relationships, so children are aware of larger numbers of more general acquaintances, of semi-anonymous people from other classes and buildings. The context of friendship in the secondary school is one in which general relationships are harder and tougher, often more brutal and invariably less personal. The desire for friendship is balanced by a need for protection:

'Well, I've got my brother and sister here, so none of them don't touch me or anything. . . . My brother and sister are tough ones. My brother's about the toughest fifth-year so he sticks up for me.'

(girl, secondary)

But individual friendships remain as significant as ever, even if blending more and more into particular groups, defined by shared attitudes and gender.[6]

Children accept school as a context in which a variety of activities take place. It is not just a place for single-minded work. It can give different kinds of satisfaction from the home. Even when lessons themselves are not proving pleasurable, dinner time or sports can become so. When children cite what it is that they most like about school they have a variety of activities to choose from. These can be aspects of classroom-based work:

> 'Well, it's because you do lots of things. Like you're able to make volcanoes and paint pictures. You can't do that at home.'
>
> (girl, primary)

Or it can be other activities as well:

> 'Yes, I quite like school for the football and the maths and sometimes we're going swimming in the summer.' (boy, primary)

Children's favourite times of the day are not usually the lessons, but the breaks between them. It is in the moments in between that they meet their friends and acquaintances, and can continue with their personal activities. This does not imply any simple dichotomy between 'boring' lessons and excitement elsewhere, since friendship is important within lessons as well as outside. Besides, children find they can continue with private pleasure within lessons and, indeed 'get out of the classroom', whatever the reason:

> 'When I'm fed up I ask if I can go to the toilet.' (girl, secondary)

Although children enjoy the breaks because of the opportunity to play with or talk to their friends, this is not the *only* time they have for this. What makes school rather different from other experiences of life is the range of activities that they undertake *with* their friends in school. Some of these take place during breaks:

> 'Playtimes. Because you get Simon tickling you in the ribs, so it's fun time. I also like games.' (boy, primary)

> 'Playtime. Because I can talk to my friends.' (girl, primary)

> 'Morning, because you get in and meet all your friends before starting work.' (boy, primary)

Despite the criticism of school meals and despite the worries over supervision, 'dinner time' features strongly as a significant moment in the child's school day. This is partly because the school day tends to be divided into a more demanding morning and less demanding afternoon; mathematics in one slot and art in the other.[7] It is also because the dinner break is the longest period of free activity within the social confines of the school:

'I like dinner time really because you can sit next to your friends and have a little chat and that makes it nice.'　　　　　(girl, primary)

(Perhaps they also enjoy the food.)

In the rituals of school life, hard work is balanced by, and sometimes contrasted with, play. Children say that they become very tired working and that they 'need the breaks'. But they would also take pleasure in the alternative activities, if they had nothing else to do all day. The breaks provide a rest, a chance to talk to friends, and also a variety of other activities children enjoy because they can be done for their own sake. The pleasure of an activity done for the pleasure it gives sometimes graces their favourite lessons. But even the most pleasurable lessons take on aspects of the way in which children use their spare time in school:

'It's nice at lunch time when the girls come in . . . just a few and we sit in class and do sewing, so we're all doing art or something and we can be together and we're part of the class.'　　　　　(girl, primary)

The desire for peace and security pervades many of the statements about school. Many of the 'best moments' show a sense of belonging, particularly to a distinct group, even a large one:

'In the Hall . . .'cos it's kind of like a family in the hall. We are all together in there.'　　　　　(boy, primary)

Security derives from a sense of cohesion within a group; it is when there is no sense of order, as in bullying, that schools become threatening.

Football is a group activity, a chance to be with others with a joint purpose. There are many enthusiasts for popular sports, and the best moments come then:

'Quarter past twelve when the football starts.'　　　　(boy, secondary)

'Lunch times. You can go and play football.'　　　　(boy, secondary)

But there are other activities:

'Riding bikes around the cycle sheds.'　　　　(girl, secondary)

The sense of taking pleasure in being in a group can be either the distinctive one of being part of a large one, as on a school trip, or the more common experience of being closely attached to a small one, like a group of girls knitting, or the particular desk in a classroom. School trips are nearly always remembered not for the reasons that they were devised, but for all the other incidents in which the children shared. Sometimes, to the chagrin of the teacher, the children recall little of the official pleasure of the art gallery or museum, but a great deal about the coach trip; the singing, or the car crash they have seen on the way. Many of the most memorable moments in the educational experience of children are those when something unusual or untoward happens, or when they feel a sense of unity with their friends:

'I've got lots of friends from my old school. The best moment was when coming back from a school trip, because of all the singing. It was good then.'   (girl, secondary)

'When we got out of school for a day . . . the bus driver was laughing.'
                                                          (boy, secondary)

Many of the pleasures of school, however, are not spectacular events that give an occasional contrast to the routine, but certain times of the day when the routine itself is peaceful. Children appreciate those quiet moments when they are not under threat, whether from the humiliation they can receive from teachers or from the bullying of other children. Just as some of the worst moments are those when they feel the strain of the work, so some of their best moments are those when this strain is alleviated, not just by escaping from the classroom but within the classroom. Lunch time is symbolic as bringing the most serious part of the day, with the heaviest load of learning, to an end. It marks a change in time:

'The afternoons, I think. Well, in the morning you get settled in to do your work and I think there are more activities in the afternoon, like games and art.'   (boy, primary)

For many children the afternoons are not only shorter and more varied but provide those moments of peacefulness which they find the most protective environment for work:

'I like to pack up everything, like I do the maths books. Packing up and after that we normally sit down and read. It's ever so quiet and peaceful.'   (boy, primary)

54

There is a close relationship between the sense of security in work and the security of being in a group. But there is also a sense of satisfaction that children derive from having worked hard, from having achieved something. There is a pleasure in steady routine:

'I like it in the middle [of the afternoon] because I'm settled down . . . at the end of the afternoon you can't wait to get home but in the middle you work.'   (girl, primary)

One of the distinct pleasures of work for children is when they have finished it, when something has been achieved and they are released from the need to apply themselves:

'In the afternoon it's a bit hard work because you've gone through the morning, and you get tired out in the afternoon. Your brain won't work . . . it's best when you've done all your work. You can choose what you want to do. Say, you're allowed to draw pictures.'

(boy, primary)

Hilary Burgess points out that teachers use different parts of the day for different purposes, and it is clear that children respond positively to the distinction.[8] They view the greater importance of some sessions over others as a reflection of their placing during the school day. Afternoons symbolize the rapid approach of the time when the work is all done, with its concomitant relaxation:

'I know it's nearly time to go home and the lessons at the end of the day are usually better than the ones at the beginning.'

(boy, secondary)

'I like the afternoons best . . . you feel more relaxed in the afternoon than you do in the mornings. You feel a bit tired in the morning.'

(girl, secondary)

The sense of having finished work is not confined only to the end of the day. For some there are clear matters of relief throughout the day:

'In between break and dinner, because there's only two lessons instead of the normal three . . . in the morning you get there, you're set your work and you can go "Ah, finish it by break," and "Ah, finished it all for the day."'   (girl, secondary)

Just as children have favourite times of the day so they have

favourite days according to the demands of the timetable.[9]
Different days bring different kinds of relief:

'Friday. You don't do too much work because you've got games after
break, then a couple of lessons and then it's PE and then you've got
the weekend to lay in.'   (boy, secondary)

Each part of the school day and the school week naturally has its
own associations in the minds of the children. For some children
the pleasure in the relief that school is over is greater than any
pleasure in school. They might be bored at home after long
holidays but accept the balance, the tension between school and
home. The possibilities of friendship are common to both.

The timetable and the curriculum appear to have a fixed
order, a cosmology of their own. There are rituals of order and
expectation, with commands given by bells and reminders
written on walls. But the impression that children give of their
experience of everyday events in school, of crowded corridors, of
friendships and gangs, of waiting and moments of escape
suggests a far more chaotic scene. Perhaps it is an inevitable
outcome of the melting pot of socialization, of the crowded nature
of the school itself, without any space for privacy. But children
notice a tendency to disorder, which remains unchecked:

'They could organize things a bit more. Like at lunch times — it's not
organized — there's just one big room and people are pushing all the
time.'   (girl, secondary)

'Everyone was chucking food and chips and things.'
                                                        (girl, secondary)

The picture of secondary schools that children carry in their
minds is of a place of bustle, of crowded corridors, of moments of
hectic rush as well as boredom. In contrast with the image of the
primary school as quiet and peaceful they think of the secondary
school as a world in which the individual must look after himself,
where the threat of being bullied is always there. In a primary
school a wilful bully can find opportunities to annoy other
children, wandering around a classroom, say, with a ruler. But in
the secondary school opportunities for hassle are thrust upon

them, and the importance of the group which has its identity outside the classroom as well as inside develops much further. Children give the impression that the transfer to secondary schools is also an initiation into a different way of thinking, into new, less gentle, relationships with other people, with both teachers and fellow pupils. The organization of lessons and of the movement of children are so different in the two types of school that children find it hard to avoid drawing attention to, and exaggerating, the different types of behaviour demanded. No longer is there the feeling of one firm centre, a classroom base, with a unified sense of purpose. The secondary school is a world that seems to children more like the unprotected world of work; of bustle caused by the movement from class to class:

> 'At first . . . you're petrified. You don't know what's going to happen or anything. . . . The moving about, things like that. You're diving off from one lesson to another lesson very fast, you find it ever so crowded in the playground . . . then there's the rush back to lessons.'
>
> (boy, secondary)

Many children express a desire for quiet places, as well as quiet moments. The desire for a 'nice place to be' remains strong in secondary schools, but the opportunities of finding such havens diminish. The opportunity of meeting friends is mitigated by the loudness of the daily routine. There are, of course, children who 'don't like being anywhere quiet because if it's quiet, it makes me all lonely' (girl, primary). Schools are far easier for those who are extrovert and can adapt to constant bustle. But the vast majority, whilst adapting to the demands of school in a pragmatic way, regret the loss of quiet places, of opportunities for less raucous dialogues. For them lessons can become havens of peace, with something to do and friends to share it with. There is no real contradiction between the dread of loneliness and the desire for quiet. For one of the main characteristics of school, especially secondary school, is the development, first of groups, or 'gangs' as Pollard would call them, and then of crowds.[10]

The social world of schools from the children's point of view is a complex mixture of individual relationships, recognition of groups and adaptation to the rituals of the establishment. The tension of school is the relationship of the individual to the

57

crowd. The fear is of being picked on, by the teacher or by a gang, and isolated. Much thought goes into working out how to form protective groups, and how to merge into a group so that no one notices. The less the individual stands out, the less the unwelcome attention from teachers and pupils. There is an underlying temptation to pick on the individual, to organize others to show their prowess by 'picking on other people' as if joining a protection racket were the only way to be protected as an individual. It is as if children are learning in their own way the powers of organization. But all share the fear of being singled out by a group, the fear of being picked on, for whatever reason:

'At first it was horrible. I didn't think it was very nice because all the people used to make fun of me because I wore glasses and I was different.'   (girl, secondary)

It is the sight of the individual being bullied that turns children's fear for themselves into something a bit more indignant, but also turns their sympathy into a relish that they themselves have escaped the bullying or the punishment:

'Some of the big kids like the third-years; there's this one girl, some of her friends call her "fatty". She doesn't frighten me but she came into class once after a boy and Miss told her off. Little John, because he's small and they all pick on him and his size and everything.'
                                                              (boy, secondary)

It is not only by teachers that children feel singled out when they are criticized or told off. The sense of personal bullying is shown in the way individual children are teased for some physical disability. Lack of popularity can come about for all kinds of reasons, and the need for friends can be prevented, for a time, by the tendency to 'gang up' against an individual, for example, one who has eczema:

'The boys still are saying "Ugh. Go away, scabby." . . . I just ignore them. But when it happened a lot in my first and second years at Juniors — in the end (you won't tell this to anybody?) — it — I feel really ashamed — I couldn't bear them picking on me — and I used to pretend I was ill, and this went on for six weeks and then my mum and the teacher cottoned on to what I was doing.
    When I first came they called me "Scabby" and things like that and

they like, weren't my friends — then — till yesterday — it was really funny — I was really surprised — I came into school and three girls came up to me and gave me Christmas cards and they said they were my friends now — it was really funny. The teachers never do nothing about it. . . .'

(girl, secondary)

Many children feel 'picked on' at times, in periods of unpopularity or being between friends. Sometimes they do not know why they are disliked, and at other times it is, to them, perfectly clear:

> 'Some of the kids are frightened of me. They think I'm a second-year, the way I look old and in a wheelchair. I look more intelligent and they get frightened.'
> (boy, secondary)

The experience of being isolated is not confined to those children whose differences draw attention to themselves. Just as the sense of unfairness is something shared by all children, so is the fear of being bullied; not just physically but in being cut off from normal dialogue with others. In their conversations with each other and their reports on such information, bullying is a phenomenon both universally recognized and generally feared. Naturally children associate bullying with secondary schools, but this is partly because there it has a more obvious physical manifestation. One of the common traumas of the transfer to secondary school is the sudden confrontation with children not only far bigger but exhibiting different patterns of behaviour. This aspect of the secondary school is part of the mythology passed back, to those about to enter:

> 'I worry definitely about the big kids in case they push you around and as soon as the bell goes you've got to rush together into another place.'
> (boy, primary)

> 'There will be lots of big children and they might boss you about a bit.'
> (girl, primary)

The bigger children are more than an incipient trepidation. They continue to be viewed with some care, having their own modes of behaviour as well as the power over smaller children:

> 'Some of the big children frighten me. Sometimes I've seen them beating each other up . . . but I'm beginning to get used to their language and things like that now.'
> (boy, secondary)

59

Some of the early fears are gradually diminished, but never at once:

> 'The first time I came here it frightened me because of all the big kids come here on their bikes but when I got to the school I was there all right.' (girl, secondary)

> 'I'm still a bit worried because I'm afraid of all the big ones a bit.' (boy, secondary)

The way to adapt to the threat of bigger children is, of course, either to avoid them, or learn how to become more like them. The lesson of organizing into groups is learned in primary school:

> 'There used to be a gang of people; if they didn't like someone they'd say they didn't like them, then the whole load of them wouldn't like them . . . and they got picked on, but in the fourth year we just stopped it. . . . We said "We can ignore it." When we were younger, we were feeble.' (girl, secondary)

But then, so is the lesson of how to survive:

> 'I was all right because I was quite tall and could pick on the other people.' (girl, secondary)

Children understand that the testing ground of some forms of relationship is bullying. Children all mention their fear of bullying in such a way that it is clear they take for granted that it will always exist. They wish teachers would do more to help control it, but they recognize that 'being picked on' and 'picking on' people are part of the social world of the school. Children seem to accept the fact that schools contain the opportunity not only for friendships but also for enmity, for violence as well as learning. Bullying appears to them to be part of the natural scene:

> 'Nothing bothers me, just probably getting smashed in by the big boys. My friend went up last year and the second day he was there he got smashed in. He didn't know why. Some boys just for the fun of it smashed him in. If we told the teachers we'd probably get smashed in after school.' (boy, primary)

Children's fear of being bullied is not based on a generalized expectation, but on particulars they have heard, on details that have been passed on to them. They are also afraid of particular boys and girls, at both primary and secondary school, who seem to pick on them. Bullying is a ritual of the corridor, a sign of group strength and identity and a result of personal enmity and grudges, an enmity the victim rarely understands. Those who are 'beaten up' do not usually know what they have done wrong or what has caused offence. But they are often confronted by the same children who pick on them and mark them out for special attention:

'Last year I didn't [enjoy school] because I had these two bullies, two girls, but they're gone now. So when I go to the comp. one of them might be there.'　　　　　　　　　　　　　　　　(girl, primary)

'They bully you . . . usually the fourth-years. It's ones that think they're big. It's just one girl at the moment who's just keeping an eye on me, sort of, like . . . I told my dad and he went round to see her so I don't think she'll do anything yet.'　　　　　　(girl, secondary)

'This girl keeps on picking on me too; she's a fourth-year.'
　　　　　　　　　　　　　　　　　　　　　　　　(boy, secondary)

The children tell of specific incidents which show how the personal attacks take place easily in the general hurly-burly of school; they highlight the many opportunities for small acts of unkindness:

'I just have to rush past that girl who bullies me. Once she thumped me and ran over my toe on her bike.'　　　　　　(girl, secondary)

'At one dinner time I was in the queue to go to have my dinner and she started on me, pushing me about and saying "You ain't there; I was there first" and all this and she kicked me.'　　(boy, secondary)

Being bullied is a ritual through which children feel they have to pass, like negotiating the rigours of the corridors. They learn, gradually, to stick up for themselves, as well as to cope:

'They didn't like me much . . . 'cos I'm so tall and some people would give me dirty looks. I just tell them to go away and if they smack me I smack them back.'　　　　　　　　　　　　　　(girl, secondary)

Children learn to adapt to the formal rules of school. They also learn the more anarchic social rules as if they were aware that they were being initiated into a different world, a counter-culture of relationships. At the formal level of schooling the relationship with the role of the teacher is important, but just as actual learning takes place at less formal levels, so children learn about social rules, and expectations, from each other. Learning who is in control and where, and learning to respect age, is part of the necessity of adaptation:

'I thought I'd be getting bullied and pushed around . . . the fifth-years have either pushed you over or something like that. It's all right as long as you keep out of their way.' (girl, secondary)

Nevertheless, for all the 'coping strategies' children realize that the bullying that goes on in the corridors is an almost impersonal, automatic thing, something that 'just happens' in school. They speak of it as if it were a ritual:

'Well, apart from trying to get to places, which has happened twice, the fifth-years have either pushed you over or something like that, like once when I went to science and the rest started to get out and they make a tunnel for you either side of the corridor and you have to try to get to the other end without falling on the floor and killing yourself. Besides that, once when I went to French this morning about six fifth-year girls sitting on the floor with their legs outstretched in front and as you try to get past they trip you over.' (girl, secondary)

Whilst certain incidents specifically come to mind, it is clear that the everyday bullying is not the same as the fearful mythology created in primary schools, but is quite palpable nevertheless:

'I was a bit scared and that when you go to lessons you nearly lose your way . . . everyone's got to go to different classrooms and you get bundled and pushed against the door, but we've all learned to push our way through now.' (boy, secondary)

The change in the measure of fear or expectation from primary to secondary school is marked not just by differences in tone or organization but by the change in the children themselves. There is a shift of emphasis from fear or anecdotes of what might happen to adapting to the facts:

'Every man for himself. As long as you stay out of their way.'
(boy, secondary)

And the children soon learn how to organize themselves, to make use of personal connections.

One of the reasons children have in seeking protection from others in secondary schools is that they find that the teachers to whom they turn for help are not interested:

'Often you go to teachers for protection and they just say "Go away" and you just get beaten up, but when you're in the class they're around you like anything if something happens . . . when you're in the upper band of school nobody's bothered, none of the teachers.'
(boy, secondary)

In the many personal vendettas engendered in groups, teachers seem to the children to play no controlling role. This is partly because some children feel it could be more dangerous if they were involved — 'If we told the teachers we'd probably get smashed up after school.' It is partly because children assume that teachers don't care:

'If you're a third-year and a fourth-year's after you, you go to the teachers for protection and they say "Go away".   (boy, secondary)

Children are sometimes bewildered at the separate world of teachers, especially when they are being initiated into the new world of the secondary school. They learn from their peer groups that teachers appear to take little interest:

'If there was a fight going on the teachers would probably hear about it and talk to the boys who did it, but one of my mates, he got beaten up by these fifth-years and the teacher hasn't done anything about it.'
(boy, secondary)

Both primary and secondary schools in their different ways are not just the creations of the teaching staff but of the children. They are the social centres in which children explore relationships with friends and enemies. Given their need to learn about fitting into social groups, it is inevitable that this is so. It is also a strong influence on more formal aspects of school, on

63

what attitudes children take towards learning and on whether they can remain 'invisible' and avoid work.[11] Children learn from each other, but they also learn about each other and observe what makes some people popular with peers and with teachers, and they see the manifestations of personal nastiness and the curious pleasure it gives to the bully. They also suffer personally from threats and isolation, as well as taking pleasure in friendly relations.

The social experience of school is equivocal. Children never see school as a place of unmitigated charm, and only rarely as a place of unrelieved misery. For virtually all children school is 'all right'. Children do not find school particularly pleasant. They might in later life think back on the best moments — 'the best days of your life'? — but are at the time conscious of the difficulties of school, the moments of terror that pervade many interviews. Their views of school show a range of equivocal opinions, changing according to the teacher and the subject, the state of relationship with their peer group, and the time of year. It is very rare to find a child, however good at work, showing unmitigated enthusiasm for school. Those who enjoy working and are successful at it are, of course, far more likely to be positive in their assessment of school, but they do discriminate between the different parts of the curriculum.

The pleasures of school are for the most part derived from the events that have only an oblique relationship to the work. One or two children express what could be considered the given, conventional view of the school, the kind of attitude that the teacher would like to hear:

> 'It teaches me a lot and I learn about what I like and the teachers are very nice and I get on well.'　　　　　　　　　　　(boy, primary)

But such a positive statement is never unmixed with some contrary doubt. Even within the same sentence children will normally make a more complex assessment. There are a few whose first response will be 'It's brilliant', but many more whose first reflection of their level of pleasure in school will be 'It's all right'. Even the more positive attitudes towards school are in a context which suggests that it is the lesser of two evils rather than something sought out. Children are simply pragmatic about the experience. Their attitudes vary according to the different activities that constitute their experience of school and according to their interest in different subjects. Their mixed feelings are expressed in their attitudes to the curriculum, and other experiences:

'I like it because there's maths groups and topic work. I'm not sure if I'd rather come to the school or go to the fair.'   (boy, primary)

'Every Wednesday you can cook and you do craft. I don't like maths. The only time I don't like school is when we break friends and we don't like each other . . . I don't like getting told off.' (girl, primary)

Children tend to blanket things that they don't like with the term 'boring'. Holidays and lessons can be 'boring'. But they also have the ability to be genuinely bored, not to know what to do with themselves. And they are as easily bored with work at school as they are fed up with home:

'Sometimes I get bored at school, sometimes when there's hard work, 'cos it's difficult to do and I get fed up when I can't do it.'

(boy, primary)

'It's all right. I can take it or leave it. . . . You get these books, right, and there's a sheet with all the questions on and you've got to find the questions in the books. It's boring. Finding the answers is boring.'

(girl, primary)

Routine lessons can strike children most unfavourably, especially in contrast to their response to new or different subjects. The lesson that seems to have no particular purpose, the need to learn facts through repetition and the demands made by a subject that they cannot grasp emerge as the dullest aspects of school life. For most of the children the worst aspect of school is not just its dullness, but the repetition of similar work, the phrase 'Do it again'. But school also has the capacity to make children fearful and anxious, both because of other children and because of teachers:

'Well, I like games but when Mr _____ does the tests at school, if we don't get eight we have to stay in and learn the words and when we've learned the words we can go out. We stay in morning break times. It's a spelling test. It's pretty frightening. You want to get them right and

65

I know children that have cried over not getting ten. Some cry in the classroom. Lately I got quite low, right, because the fourth-year words I get are quite hard. The third-years have their words. Spelling is difficult. I've had a cry, but on my own. I don't let anybody see. Sometimes I like maths.'   (girl, primary)

There are many children for whom the routine of school includes regular measure of such fear, not fear of the punishments meted out but fear of the sense of failure and humiliation.

Children's attitudes to school are not, therefore, of a conventionally rosy sort. They accept the institutions and understand how they work as well as having a clear sense of what they are for. But they also know that schools have potential for misery as well as pleasure. The result is that their feelings about school are both complicated and neutral.

'We've got enjoyable things about it . . . sometimes I just pick it up easily. I don't pick up maths too easily but sometimes I do . . . sometimes I don't feel like school and that's when I go right off and my writing gets messy but that's when I've had an early night.'

(boy, primary)

'It's all right. Well, I don't enjoy it, but it's all right.

(boy, secondary)

The question is, could we expect more of an accolade than that?

NOTES AND REFERENCES

1. Davies, B. *Life in the Classroom and Playground: The Accounts of Primary School Children.* London: Routledge and Kegan Paul, 1982.
2. For the *uses* of this in learning see the later chapters.
3. Pollard, A. *The Social World of the Primary School.* London: Holt, Rinehart and Winston, 1985.
4. Cullingford, C. *Parents, Teachers and School.* London: R. Royce, 1986, Chapter 8.
5. Davies (*op cit.*) calls them 'functional'.
6. Rubin, Z. *Children's Friendships.* Wells: Open Books, 1980.
7. Burgess, H. 'The primary curriculum: the example of mathematics.' In C. Cullingford, *The Primary Teacher.* London: Cassell, 1989, pp. 16–36.
8. *Ibid.*
9. Sales, M. 'Pupil perspectives on the first year curriculum.' Diploma in Curriculum Development, Oxford Polytechnic, 1986.
10. Pollard, *op cit.*
11. See Pye, J. *Invisible Children: Who Are the Real Losers at School?* Oxford: Oxford University Press, 1989.

CHAPTER 6
School Rules and Discipline

'If you didn't have rules in the school, everybody'll just be running
riot.'
(boy, primary)

Children in schools create their own rules of relationships. The
fluid way in which they form groups or gangs and the parts that
they play within classes are all governed by implicit rules. But
these are embedded in a framework that the institutions impose
upon them. The opportunities for indiscipline, as in the
corridors, are nevertheless controlled by overall expectations in
the schools. The school, as an autonomous organization, creates
its own set of rules without which it could not function.
Obedience to these is one of the cardinal virtues. When children
tell each other about different teachers, and analyse their
response to bullying, they detect the gap between the ostensible
rules and the degree to which these rules can be broken. Even
during initiation into a secondary school, let alone in primary
schools, children learn how to subvert rules, or ignore them, how
to test them and when to apply them.[1]

Just as children have dual attitudes to relationships, so they
hold complex attitudes to school rules. There is a general context
in which children need to understand the basis for the teachers'
authority.[2] They need to place such understanding in a
framework of society, with its police forces and systems of
punishment. But children also test out the personal face of such
authority, to see whether such authority, in the personality of the
teacher, can be manipulated. So their relationship with teachers
can become personal examinations of role and explorations of
how far roles can be made personal.[3] Children are soon aware of
the existence of school rules, implicit as well as explicit, and
aware of their fragility. They also explore different ways of
responding to the rules, by 'teasing' and attention-seeking, or
remaining obscure.[4] Schools are, after all, meeting places where
friendships and enemies are formed, and therefore tested.[5] All
social relationships depend on a framework of rules, of shared
expectations and understandings.

Children accept that their happiness depends as much on their relationships with other children as on their experience of being taught formally. But they also accept the fact that schools depend on a clear sense of discipline and a sense of order. Even while they test it, children acknowledge the authority of teachers in imposing this order. Indeed, children express a very strong sense of the need for strict rules and firm discipline. They invariably criticise a school or teacher for being too lax, or inconsistent, rather than too firm. They think there should be more rules than less. Why?

In their acceptance of the school rules and regulations and the need for imposed discipline children are more closely in tune with their parents' attitudes than with those expressed by teachers.[6] It is parents who most clearly express the view that it is the school's function to discipline children, to teach them codes of behaviour:

'I hope she gets a certain amount of discipline from school. I think that's important.'

The parents also ache for more discipline; they feel, like the children, that if there are faults in schools they lie on the side of too much leniency rather than too firm a rule of law:

'Let's face it; schools have relaxed discipline too much.'

'I think they should be more stricter in school than they are.'

Children believe in rules, not only their own implied ones but those, however seemingly trivial, promulgated by schools. They are strong believers in discipline, in having rules imposed on them and firmly carried out. This is because, as their statements demonstrate, they believe that they learn by being told how to do things. They do not assume that goodness is innate, an autonomous sense of innocence preserved. They think that it is only by learning social behaviour that people are prevented from doing harm. They presume that self-discipline and moral behaviour are a product of outside forces; of rules that they must learn. To this extent children do not share with teachers the liberal idea that they will naturally express a gift for kindly relationships. They do, in their own way, learn what teachers call social autonomy.[7] But they do so in *reaction* to all that is around them.

Children stand firm in the belief that they need to have rules imposed upon them, that these rules are necessary or else there would be chaos, and that these rules should be clearly communicated and strictly enforced. The relationship between their sense of the school as a structure of enforceable rules and their own complicated social aspirations is a fairly ambiguous one but it appears that children see the school both as sharing their values and as equally determinedly controlling their actions.[8]

The teacher's role is partly that of imposing rules and making sure that the rules are enforced. This is to protect those whom rules are designed to serve — the weak — from those who children assume will try to break the rules — the strong. It is a telling and oft-repeated comment of children that rules are the only barrier against extreme bullying and natural excess. Without such rules how would the weaker ones survive?

'They'll need a lot of rules because the big people are not allowed to boss the first-years around. . . . Teachers are . . . always there to tell you off and that.' (boy, primary)

'Rules are to protect us and young children . . . if a child has been brought up wrong and inflicts pain, he'll have to have stricter rules.' (girl, primary)

The importance of teachers lies not so much in the fact that they create and communicate rules but in the fact that they have the sanctions to impose the rules. They are the ones who hold the ultimate power, who make the manifestations of rules clear in punishments:

'It's up to the teachers if the children have been bad or not.' (boy, secondary)

'Because if they don't the class would be mucking around all the time.' (girl, secondary)

Greater prominence is given to rules in secondary schools by children because they assume that people grow more wicked as they get older. This implies the need for a growing scale of punishments. They make the assumption that the older the child the more fierce the threat and scale of punishment should be.

69

Although most children see the necessity for harsher rules in secondary schools, they are also aware of their growing ability to adapt to them. The reason for their belief in greater strictness derives from the fact that younger children are clearly perceived as more easily cajoled or frightened by being told off. As they get older so something more palpable, like detention, is felt to be necessary because of the growing ability to bypass or ignore rules. But even strict punishments can be taken in their stride, so that whatever the type of sanction, the child can deal with it:

> 'Well, they're both the same really, because at the primary you got a really big telling off, but here you only get told off a little bit and then you just get a detention, so really that's getting off fairly light.'
>
> (boy, secondary)

The existence of rules is essential. Occasionally the interpretation of rules by a particular teacher may be unfair, but the necessity for them is never in question. There are no complaints about the rules themselves, and the children go out of their way to suggest that they are fair as well as necessary:

> 'Yes, the rules are fair because they keep behaviour in the school . . . it makes the school much nicer.' (girl, primary)

> 'That's a discipline and you find that after a while you're better with discipline . . . it's fair, for what you've done there should be a penalty for it.' (boy, secondary)

If the rules are fair, as children keep insisting, they also imply that punishments are fair, whether being told off or put into detention. As long as it is clear what the rules and punishments are then almost anything can be taken on board:

> 'One rule is "Do your homework", that is "make sure that you've done that and that you're up with the others". . . . If you don't you're punished. It's fair if you haven't done it.' (girl, secondary)

The social and moral assumption that as people grow older so they grow more wicked and more difficult to control creates an increasing need for rules:

> 'Rules are for safety here, There'll be lots of rules and they'll be different at the secondary. You'd be killed and that if there wasn't. There'll be stricter rules.' (girl, primary)

The larger the children and the bigger the school, the clearer is the need for firmness and sanctions:

> 'We have school rules and they're fair. One of them is not to fight, because if you go around fighting or stealing when you get older you're going to go around doing it again.'　　　　　(girl, primary)

That puts the need for rules firmly in its place: the expectation that children learn by being told what to do. But they also assume that:

> 'There'll be harder rules, because there's a lot more people to take care of. They'll make them a lot harder to understand.'
>
> (boy, primary)

Not all children seemed to think that once a lesson is taught it stays taught. On the contrary, the opportunities for breaking rules, as well as creating more of them, seemed so much greater in the secondary school:

> 'There'll be more rules at the comp. because there's more people. When you go for different lessons there'll be so many people moving about they'll be knocking everybody over.'　　　　(girl, primary)

> 'They'll be stricter. There's a lot more children there, . . . and there'll be more trouble.'　　　　　　　　　　　　　　(boy, primary)

Although the secondary school children, facing and experiencing a far wider range of punishments, were more pragmatic about rules, they show no signs of disagreeing with the primary school children's picture of their future school experience as being bound up by more rules, and by the need for even more rules:

> 'They have to learn. If you can't trust them you'll have to punish them or tell them they can't be trusted. There'll be a lot more children at the comp. and so you'll have rules for different classes.'
>
> (boy, primary)

> 'School rules are all right. I can remember them all. . . . The teachers will keep telling you off as . . . if you're naughty you deserve it. The people are older there so you need more rules. They might be vandals.'　　　　　　　　　　　　　　　(girl, primary)

Never do we seem to meet the expectation that with maturity will

71

come greater self-control, improved behaviour or more natural kindness to others. In fact all the children seem to assume that rules continue to be necessary because children do *not* learn. The primary school children look with awe at the wilder antics of some pupils at secondary school and fear this behaviour will steadily get worse as their peer groups grow older. But this is almost a moral assumption, not only about learning but about human behaviour. They suggest that it is natural to be wicked and that without strict rules this wickedness would be demonstrated:

> 'If you didn't have rules in the school, everybody'll just be running riot . . . they may have some kids who turn out really to be naughty, so you'll need more rules.'   (boy, primary)

> 'The children would be bad if there wasn't rules . . . and everybody would do just what they wanted to . . . they'll have to be stricter because they've got a lot more people to keep an eye on.'
> (girl, primary)

> 'If we're out of order all hell would break loose.'   (girl, secondary)

Children's views of human nature seem bleakly conservative. They do not envisage a time when self-restraint or a natural sense of order will make rules unnecessary. They clearly see the need for the imposition of rules, for careful control, for the sake of avoiding 'chaos' and for the needs of work:

> 'They'll be much stricter and they'll be older. Older children need stricter rules because when you get older you get cheeky and everything.'   (boy, primary)

> 'The rules will be harder and stricter. They'll be harder to keep. Stricter rules will help you get your work done.'   (girl, primary)

> 'If we didn't have school rules this place would be upside down. If we didn't have the rules everybody would be naughty and the school would be untidy and messy.'   (boy, primary)

Children are unified in their agreement about the natural depravity of human nature. They seem to accept that the condition of being a pupil, rather than an adult, necessitates the imposition of sanctions, almost as if they were expected to test the rules or those who impose them. One or two children suggest, rather sadly, that:

> 'When you get to the comp. you should be old enough to know better, but the punishments will be harder.' (girl, primary)

but they do not really expect any actual improvement in behaviour to take place. In the secondary school they have got used to a series of rules and punishments, and they are especially conscious of the latter. When they say that the rules are fair, they take for granted that they are necessary to maintain order. Their comments therefore concentrate on the ways in which retribution and the threats of retribution are administered.

Children think of rules as a necessary series of sanctions, as social control of the natural tendency to behave badly. Rules are not just a series of suggestions that need to be remembered for the good of all. They need to be remembered because children would otherwise get into trouble. The children believe in their necessity in such a way as to suggest that it is the rules themselves that must be made clear and not the moral behaviour implicit in the rules. Rules are there, after all, to be tested. It is taken for granted that they will be disobeyed by many. The consequences of breaking the rules and being found out are themselves fascinating for children and much energy is given to the exploration of why sanctions are sometimes imposed on different children by different teachers inequitably. But the rules are accepted as the only means of organizing a large number of pupils, and are observed to be a necessary preparation for later life:

> 'If you don't keep the rules, it won't help you when they get tougher later on in your life.' (boy, primary)

> 'If we didn't have rules we could come to school any time we wanted. If we didn't have rules you'd get up to all sorts of mischief.'
> (girl, primary)

> 'You wouldn't be under control if you hadn't rules.' (boy, primary)

> 'We have rules because someone might get hurt.' (girl, primary)

73

Children see rules as the means of preventing things going wrong, rather than positive encouragements towards good behaviour. No one mentions any association between rules and doing good, or being well behaved. Children are pragmatic about the particular purposes of rules. The fabric of the building needs protection.

The purposes of control are interpreted in terms not only of pupils' behaviour but of the protection of property:

> 'Well, yes, there's a lot of rules. Yes, we have to have rules. Rules like tidying up the school are very important because if people come along and see the school is all messy it wouldn't be any good.'
>
> (girl, primary)

> 'Detention's fair . . . because all people do here is making it untidy and just when I come here people kept setting off alarms and breaking the glass . . .'
>
> (girl, secondary)

Rules are part of the ethos of the school. Children view the remembering of rules as one of the main tasks of initiation. The teacher's task is to enable the children to remember all the rules. Many children point out that they can 'remember' all of them; others are uncertain whether they are aware of every one. Guilt lies more in knowing them and disobeying them than in carrying out the same actions without realizing that they were specifically prohibited. It is therefore important in children's eyes to know the rules and be able to rehearse them. After all, they hear them often enough both in and outside lessons:

> 'On the tannoy they tell you things.'
>
> (boy, secondary)

> 'I don't flood the toilets because people keep flooding the toilets and she said "Don't get the things out until I tell you" and all that. When we go to PE we've got to be very quiet because down the corridor there's other classes working, so if we make a noise we have to go back again. Anyhow, I take it as it comes.'
>
> (boy, secondary)

> 'Not to eat in class, not to run, it's nearly all the same rules really because you're not allowed to shout across the class or anything; you have to put up your hand.'
>
> (girl, secondary)

Rules are often rehearsed, repeated and insisted upon. They are kept in children's minds because the punishments are a constant reminder:

> 'They are quite easy to remember. I think they'll be stricter. I think there's punishments. I hope I'll remember the rules. I hope I don't get punishments.' (boy, primary)

Children have a fairly flexible attitude to their personal experience, in which the sanctions against disobedience are taken almost as a necessary part of the rules rather than as the desire to create a clear moral and social order:

> 'It's fair, for which you've done there should be a penalty for it.' (boy, secondary)

> 'punishments . . . it doesn't really make you regret it or anything. It just makes you worried; you're always worrying.' (girl, secondary)

Punishments themselves not only seem to carry little moral obloquy but are regarded pragmatically:

> 'You'd just get shouted at, told off, perhaps sent to the headmaster, if you're really bad.' (boy, secondary)

Having detentions, being punished, is clearly a natural part of school life for many, as is being bullied. There are few hints of ambivalence about the system:

> 'You'd get detention and all that . . . fair . . . yes, if it's that, but there shouldn't be punishment.' (girl, secondary)

For the most part the system, like the examination system, is taken for granted, including physical punishment as if it were still a part of the system. A few children even feel that there is still an important place for the cane, as the ultimate deterrent:

> 'You're in trouble . . . you either get detention, taken to the headmaster or caned, but the cane's been banned . . . not a good thing for some of the fifth-years that swear . . . we ought to have it back.' (boy, secondary)

or because it seems a more sensible last resort than suspension:

> 'Maybe the cane . . . because if they're suspended they'll lose a lot of education and they might be going down to the shops and doing all kinds of things.' (boy, secondary)

Although the cane is banned it is still associated in children's minds with the final deterrent, and with those activities most likely to demand strict measures:

'My big brother in comp. — he mainly doesn't do his homework when he gets home. Well, if I don't do mine properly, I'll get the cane.' (girl, primary)

'Well, there should be rules for the quiet area. . . . My big brother's friend, he swore at the headmaster at comp. and he got the cane. He was swearing at the teachers and the headmaster. We don't get the cane here. My big brother, about two weeks ago, was thumping people.' (girl, primary)

Children are phlegmatic about rules. They do not expect the rules of which they approve to be universally kept. They also assume that teachers will keep imposing more rules if necessary and finding new punishments if the 'normal' ones do not work. At the same time children expect teachers to obey their side of the bargain and impose the rules not leniently but fairly. One of the great anguishes about childhood is the sense of outrage when something is unfair. Given the rigid system of checks and balances, of rules and punishments, this is not surprising. But rarely, if ever, do children suggest that the system itself is unfair:

'That's about all the rules. You get suspended. I don't know if it's fair. Some people go about telling tales and get done for it. You still get detention and that's not fair.' (boy, primary)

'It's fair, unless you never did it. I said I didn't do it. Sometimes they said I did and I just got accused.' (boy, secondary)

Part of the annoyance children feel when the system does not work is with other children who put their fellows into trouble:

'Some boys in my class, they make up fibs to get the other person into trouble for doing nothing. . . . It'll get worse there.' (girl, primary)

Another sense of unfairness is with the teacher who cannot tell the difference between truth and falsehood and therefore seems indifferent. Only occasionally do we find a more subtle questioning of such a system:

'What teachers say to us and over the tannoy, what people keep saying to us . . . the problem is that Tracey, Tina and I, we kept being late because we waited for the doors to open . . . and we kept being late and got a detention for doing that . . . I don't reckon that's fair really because Mr ___'s late sometimes and we can't exactly give him detention, can we?' (girl, secondary)

But the rules for teachers are quite another matter.

Children recognize the school as a hierarchy of power in which teachers are in a necessary authority over them. They accept that teachers make the law and that its rule is important, if not absolute. 'Even if they do not think the interpretation of rules always fair, they accept the given order as inevitable. This view of authority underlies children's general views of school. Their views of human nature are conservative. They sense that without close supervision and control, anything might happen, given people's propensity for making mischief. This acceptance of the necessity for rules reflects their view of society and the school as a microcosm of society. Like society as depicted on television, a school is a hierarchical organization, with teachers as significant figures and with the headteacher as the ultimate authority.[9]

To children schools cannot survive without strong control. Whether this is a matter of supervising corridors when necessary or quietening the classroom, the implicit structure of the school is not so much an agreed acceptance of a common purpose and the sharing of responsibilities as of handing out instructions and encouragement, punishment and reward, from the few to the many. This might seem an obvious description of a school, but we sometimes forget what it is actually like to be in such circumstances.

In such a hierarchy the headteacher is almost automatically a figure of awe and distance, as authoritative as the idea of a prime minister and much more immediate. The fact that children rarely make comments on the headteacher as a person is in itself significant. It is as if the head were beyond the normal everyday concerns of children. Yet there is a sense of the presence of such a figure who, even if unapproachable, provides at least a space outside her study and who gives the fiercest punishments. The head is also the person who organizes and controls what teachers do. The children feel more than just respect for the head:

'I didn't like going to the headmaster. . . . I've never been to him before but he just gives me the creeps.' (girl, secondary)

77

The larger the school the less chance there is of seeing the headteacher but even in primary schools the headteacher is a figure of power rather than immediacy. Whilst one can think of exceptions because of the size of the school and the personal manner of individuals, this conception seems to be deeply entrenched in children's minds. Whatever the casualness of manner affected by the headteacher, she is, in children's eyes, by virtue of her office, the person who wields control. She is the person ultimately responsible for punishment and the one to avoid being told off by:

> 'The head . . . he's quite angry most of the time when he walked about and if you got him on the wrong end you got told off quite badly.' (boy, secondary)

The headteacher, then, wields authority (in children's eyes literally) and is associated with the law and order of the school. It is true that the secondary head is more invisible and is even less likely to be met in the role of a class teacher. It is also true that the secondary headteacher's room is more likely to be, both in place and fact, less welcoming to parents. It is also the case that there are hierarchies in secondary schools, like year tutors and heads of departments, that make the distant head a more awesome figure, just as the school as a whole is. But the perception of children rightly sees that the similarities are greater than the differences. Headteachers in both primary and secondary schools are financial managers, responsible to governors, implementing a state-controlled curriculum. They are bound to their desks, and supported by secretarial staff. And, crucially, they have the final sanction of responsibility for their own staff. The headteacher is the person the child is sent to when all else has failed.

Supported by such authority, the class teachers are responsible for keeping order, and need to accept such a role to be credible. But they are also expected to impose order, even when the children are testing their ability to do so. At least children *want* the teacher to win the battle for order:

> 'You don't want classes with everyone jumping around.' (boy, secondary)

''cos if everyone runs around people who want to work won't get the chance to . . . most teachers do keep good order.' (girl, secondary)

And yet, whilst imposing order, the teacher must juxtapose authority with individual help. For children expect the rules to cover, when possible, the bullying that is inflicted on the individual:

> 'If I get into trouble, I tell her about it so she can clear it up. I don't know if I'll be able to talk to my teacher at secondary school.'
>
> (boy, primary)

As we have noted, children see the limitations of teacher's powers of, or interests in, intervention. But whilst in the classroom, whatever distance is held from the turbulence of children's play times, teachers exert a subtle form of control through giving rewards:

> 'She'd usually keep on choosing you to do things. There were some people at our last school who kept getting choosed for things.'
>
> (girl, secondary)

Children know that all is going well when they are encouraged and praised or when they avoid trouble:

> 'They smile at me.' (girl, secondary)

> 'I haven't been shouted at many times, and I'm sometimes asked questions and that.' (boy, secondary)

Maintaining a good relationship with a teacher is part of the art of mastering the rules, which sometimes work as subtly as the complex relationships with peers.

In a primary school a lot depends on the intricacies of the relationship with the class teacher. In the secondary school the intricacies of the battle for power are more complex. The primary classroom is dominated by a series of individual relationships. In the secondary school there is a greater stress on collective strategies, both in pupils and staff. Measor and Woods[10] describe an episode in a comprehensive school in which discipline began to fall apart through the ability of some of the children to assert themselves, find an audience and push back the frontiers of sanctions and control to the point at which the staff felt so threatened that they deliberately began a campaign to 'squash' the threatened indiscipline. Both sides saw the essential parameters of the relationship as a struggle for control, a struggle which the teachers won, but a struggle nevertheless.

Although children accept the authority of the school they are not subservient to it. They feel the need to challenge it. What is surprising is not so much the fact that children are potentially in a state of constant battle with teachers, so that teachers have to know as much about harbouring emotional energy as harbouring knowledge, but that the children do finally accept the school's authority. There are truants, and some children who upset the normal order, but children in the primary schools and in the early years of secondary schools do not question their position very deeply. As children become older so the relationships and a sense of hierarchy become more complex. Instead of an underlying sense of friends in each other and in teachers, children become aware of ranks of teachers, difficult relationships between them, layers of intermediate control in which the teachers, in the perception of a child in school, have better things to do than to talk to the individual pupil:

> 'I don't think we'll be able to talk to the teacher at the comp. as much as we can in the primary school, because the people up there have bigger responsibilities than here.' (boy, primary)

One assumption made about the class teacher is that she needs to be an expert at class control and class management.[11] Whilst acknowledging the great complexity of running an operation that is interesting and demanding to thirty individuals, this is a curious assumption. It means that the teacher is not seen to be a fount of knowledge or delivery of the curriculum, to whom pupils come for enlightenment, but as a controller of recalcitrant, unwilling children, with all the emotional strain that implies.

And yet for children this is the essential ethos of the school. They accept the need for rules, for the sanctity of discipline. But they also assume that they have, up to a point, the right to challenge it. They consider that it is the natural propensity of people to be bad, and that teachers are therefore needed to impose discipline. For some philosophers discipline arises out of a sense of guilt, and out of moral concern. It depends on an understanding of the need for self-awareness and authority. For children the rules of school are based not on moral guilt but on fear of punishment, not so much on self-restraint as on commands. This also becomes part of children's vision of society as a whole.

NOTES AND REFERENCES

1. McManus, M. *Troublesome Behaviour in the Classroom*. London: Routledge, 1989.
2. Wilson, J. and Cowell, B. *Children and Discipline: A Teacher's Guide*. London: Cassell, 1990.
3. Cronk, J.K. *Teacher–Pupil Conflict in Secondary Schools*. Lewes: Falmer Press, 1988.
4. Sluckin, A. *Growing up in the Playground*. London: Routledge and Kegan Paul, 1981.
5. Goodnow, J. and Burns, A. *Home and School: A Child's Eye View*. London: Allen and Unwin, 1985.
6. Cullingford, C. *Parents, Teachers and Schools*. London: Robert Royce, 1986, Chapter 8.
7. *Ibid.*
8. Lee, P.C., Statuto, C.M. and Kedar-Voivadas, G. 'Elementary school children's perceptions of their actual and ideal school experience: a developmental study.' *Journal of Educational Psychology*, **75** (6), 838-847, 1983.
9. Wilson and Cowell, *op.cit.*
10. Measor, L. and Woods, P. *Changing Schools: Pupil Perspective on Transfer to a Comprehensive*. Milton Keynes: Open University Press, 1984.
11. DES *Discipline in Schools*. Report of the Committee of Enquiry chaired by Lord Elton. London, 1989.

CHAPTER 7
Teachers and their Teaching Styles

'I like his lessons, but I don't like him.' (girl, secondary)

The social world of school is dominated in numbers by the mass of pupils, their talk, their work and their movements. But the ethos of the school is presented through teachers. Teachers dominate in a subtle way. Their effect on the way the school runs, on how the children work and on children's happiness is profound.[1] This dominance is conveyed in an indirect way. The sense of purpose amongst teachers is rarely spelled out, and there is a gap between expressed intentions and daily actions. Indeed, it is through the half-hidden assumptions with which they go about their business that teachers make their mark on children. There can even be a conflict between what teachers think they are doing and what they are actually doing.[2] Teachers can present a far more muddled or complex picture of their expectations than they think they are presenting.[3] From the children's point of view teachers are a constant source of study, partly because of this difference between avowed intention and behaviour.

In children's analysis of teachers there is a clear tension between the personality of the individual teacher and the impersonal authority of the position. Schools are understood as embodiments of the teacher's will. They convey, in their fabric and organization, what teachers think is important. Whether in the reception areas or in the closed staffroom, teachers present an aspect of their self-image and the ethos of the school, for the two are closely connected. Children accept the role of teachers and although they can sometimes rebel against it, they submit to the realities of power. That is why any rebellion tends to be individual, or subtle. Authority is ignored rather than challenged, bypassed rather than confronted.

The reason why children exhibit less obvious forms of deviance is that they accept the role of authority carried by the teacher, but realize that the role is imposed on an individual personality.

For every teacher, especially at the beginning of her career, there is a conflict between the desire to be liked, to respond to individual human beings, and the need to impose an abstract order on the group. Children understand this tension. They know how teachers can be undermined, and when a teacher means what she says. They always understand the personality beneath the role.

Because of the nature of their jobs, teachers create a habit of working which is both emotionally strenuous and unlike any other. Teachers' uses of language have often been parodied, since they need to convey moral authority, which can sound patronizing, and since they need to insist on order, which can sound absurd. Teachers use a language that would not be used elsewhere. The use of rhetorical questions as commands — 'Are we going to be quiet?' — and the use of words as signals for change — 'right' is the word that teachers in Britain use most, meaning anything from 'stop' to 'listen' from 'be quiet' to 'start working' — are uses of language grounded in schools. Children learn a variety of codes, and the distinctions between the uses of language in personal dialogue and as a vehicle for public announcements.

Children have an equivocal attitude to teachers because of this mixture of personality and role. They are clear about what they appreciate in teachers and what they dislike, but find very few either wholly good or wholly bad. They spend a significant amount of their time assessing teachers and spreading the word about those that other children have not yet met.[4]

But they all have to establish their own relationships:

'When I first came, when I looked at all the tutors, I wanted Miss L. 'cos she looked, you know, the most unstrict. And when I looked at Mr P., he looked strict and I hoped I didn't have him — and when I turned out to have him, I went "Oh No!" and then I found out he was a right softie.'   (girl, secondary)

The need to establish personal relationships means that children look for consistency. They need to know what the teacher will demand in her role of authority, and how far she will respond as a person. They take time to understand particular teachers' foibles:

'After a while you know what the teacher's like and you can go up and ask them and you'll know that they'll help you.'   (boy, primary)

Children find it difficult if they do not know where they stand and if the teacher has sudden, inexplicable changes of mood.

In primary schools children have time to assess their teachers and most of the assumptions about them remain unspoken. But in secondary schools children find it necessary to pass on judgements, to convey reputations. The analysis is not so much a personal one but a question of which idiosyncrasies are significant, which teacher can be cajoled into wasting time, and which teacher cannot be trusted. Much of the attention children pay is to their weaknesses, their lack of control or inability to explain. Teachers are both respected and analysed, feared and taken for granted. Children develop a laconic view of their behaviour:

'Sometimes you get the odd teacher shouting.'   (boy, secondary)

They have a strong sense of the role of the teacher, and the need for distance as well as friendliness:

'I would trust a teacher, but I would talk to my friends.'
(boy, primary)

They also observe the difference between the standards of behaviour that teachers expect of them and the standards they apply to themselves. They resent the occasions when teachers do not follow their own rules. But they know that teachers will continue with their *own* codes of behaviour:

'She's a bit bossy, and a bit, you know, a bit . . . she don't talk to people, you know, the way we have to talk to them, like. We have to say please, and she didn't say please like we have to say please.'
(boy, secondary)

Children like, but do not always expect, consistency. They know that each teacher will do things differently so that there is not one set standard of behaviour. Some teachers, for example, will be more friendly than others:

'I think I'm popular with my own teacher. I know that. It's embarrassing. She comes past and winks at me. She comes round and calls me love, and asks me to do things . . . I don't know why I'm popular with people.'   (boy, primary)

Such friendliness is itself an inconsistency, for teachers are meant to be as distant as they are friendly and the reputation that is conveyed of them at secondary school is pervasive:

> 'Hmm . . . teachers. You hear things about the teachers up here. You hear they are pretty hard and things like that. My brother tells me the teachers are grumpy.'　　　　　　　　　　　　　　(boy, primary)

Teachers have a distinct place of their own. The whole tenor of the relationship is not be be confused with any other. Teachers are friendly, but not friends. Teachers are to be tested as well as obeyed. The importance of being liked is that it prevents being 'picked on'. 'I'm not one of their favourites' (girl, secondary). Friendships are explored with other children and the types of behaviour appropriate in one set of circumstances is not deemed appropriate in another:

> 'I haven't told my teacher yet but she knows there's a lot of silly boys around because one came in and he was talking to her and the words, the language he used, and the way he slouched around!'
>
> 　　　　　　　　　　　　　　　　　　　　　　　　　　(girl, secondary)

Teachers are looked at equivocally. They impose both collective and idiosyncratic rules, and children need to adapt to them:

> 'There's one teacher that's different from the rest. In other classes we have to ask permission to take our jackets off, but Mr A., if he takes his jacket off we can take ours off without asking him, but if he's got his on we have to ask to take ours off.'　　　　　(girl, secondary)

The behaviour of teachers *needs* to be observed as it has an impact on the children. But in the end children accept, as well as analyse, the behaviour of teachers. There is an almost laconic air to the realization that teachers will have their funny moods:

> 'He just goes nuts ... don't really bother me, really.'
>
> 　　　　　　　　　　　　　　　　　　　　　　　　　　(boy, secondary)

> 'They have their little moans occasionally and then you just get on with your work.'　　　　　　　　　　　　　　　　(boy, secondary)

The teacher who oversteps the boundaries of teacher–pupil relationships can be as embarrassing as the teacher who reveals too clearly personal frailty or personal animosity. But all children want to be liked, and they want to like their teachers. Success in work depends on a sense of confidence that is nurtured by belief and fostered by praise. The teacher's willingness to take an interest in individual work leads not only to confidence but to an appreciation of the teacher. In this way the 'good' teacher, in her knowledge of individual children's needs, becomes 'nice':

> 'The work's fun . . . because the teacher is nice and if you had a teacher who was horrible you wouldn't want to get on and learn and if you've got a nice teacher it's easier to learn.'　　　(girl, primary)

The atmosphere in which children work obviously affects them and the 'nice' teacher is one who can create it. The classroom then becomes a relaxed place:

> 'I like to have my own classroom . . . and my own teacher because you're younger now and it's much more cosy to stay in one place most of the time and you don't get fed up with the teacher.'
>
> 　　　(boy, primary)

If there is an atmosphere which is conducive to learning, then the familiarity with a teacher is central. Children resent feeling belittled, through sarcasm or through indifference to their work. The 'nice' teacher is encouraging and expresses infinite patience with children's learning:

> 'She's ever so good because if any of us do anything wrong, she doesn't get annoyed about it, she just kind of says, "Don't worry".'
>
> 　　　(girl, primary)

This kind of teacher is also consistent, so children know what to expect. They do not resent the teacher being strict. In fact 'niceness' is often allied to strictness; children do not think of the two as contrasts:

> 'She was ever so hard. She's the sort of teacher I like — kind. I don't mind her being strict because she was kind. Mrs B. was terrible, she used to take it out on us.'　　　(girl, primary)

Children want to like their teachers and generally want to be liked in return. They are usually clear about where they stand in the teacher's eyes. Teachers cannot help showing their feelings to some extent and making it apparent whom they like and whom they don't. They also know how to manipulate as well as display their feelings. Children observe signs of different moods, and judge when teachers take an interest. They also hope to see encouragement in the teacher's demeanour towards them:

> 'If you're naughty she speaks deeply and when she looks happy she likes you. She always looks happy at me.' (boy, primary)

> 'I'm quite happy here because Mrs P. likes me and she likes giving me responsibility. That's how I know she likes me and she doesn't shout at me a lot when I've done something wrong. She tells me off but that's not too bad. She explains why I shouldn't do it.'
> (girl, primary)

The feeling of being liked is tempered by the knowledge that such liking is negotiated. It is dependent on the mutual contract of work; that teacher and pupil will perform in agreed ways. It does not matter how strictness is balanced by encouragement, but it is the balance that creates the working atmosphere:

> 'She'd feel sorry for me and she kept cuddling me. If anything happened to me she'd care. It's OK if you work for them.'
> (boy, primary)

These are two particular signs of a 'nice' teacher. One characteristic of a teacher who creates comfortable relationships is a sense of humour:

> 'Mr C. puts bits of fun into it and if you finish your work you can do nice things.' (girl, primary)

> 'It's nice in Mr D's class. He always make jokes and things.'
> (boy, secondary)

The other is the sense that teachers can 'join in', that they do not remain so exclusive as to be uninterested in what children are doing:

> 'Mrs H. always takes us for country dancing and she always joins in. And she joins in games as well, which is quite nice really. It makes us better. . . . The teacher makes it nice because she joins in with things with us.' (girl, primary)

The sense of the primary classroom as a happy and comfortable place is because of the atmosphere created by a friendly teacher but most children do not want the teacher to be exclusive to them. They wish to see the teacher willing to act the part in an open and humorous manner, so that there is a collective atmosphere of pleasure in which all can join:

> 'you know you gotta like him — he's our teacher, he's all right, not bad. When someone makes a joke up — Michael, he makes a lot of jokes up — he makes a funny grin on his face.'   (boy, secondary)

> '. . . and he made jokes all the time. He put you in a good mood for the day. He was once telling someone off for calling someone else names — and he was saying, you know, "sticks and stones will break your bones" and we all start chorusing, and he laughed. Good teachers always make you feel sort of, more welcome.'
>
> (girl, secondary)

The popular teacher creates an atmosphere in which children enjoy their work. For 'humour' and 'joining in' are not seen as alternatives to work but ways of making the necessary work more rewarding. There are a number of ways in which children feel the teachers' interest. Many children single out the pleasures of seeing their work displayed:

> '. . . and I'm better because Mrs ____ encourages me and I can draw much better now. She puts my things on the wall. Every time my Mum and Dad have been to see my work my things have been on the wall.'   (boy, primary)

> 'We do weather charts and if we get them up to date they go on the walls, on show. Your parents, when they come on open evening, can see you've been trying hard and doing good things.' (girl, primary)

The sense of being publicly praised, of having something to show, seems to children to be a result of the teacher's interest. It is also a sign that the teacher is aware of the world outside the classroom, of the individual child and not, exclusively, the task they are undertaking:

> 'We read aloud to the teacher so she knows what I'm like at reading and she can let the other school know what I'm like.' (girl, primary)

Such public confidence, and the displays of success can seem almost like a bribe. If they work hard then there will be a commensurate amount of relaxation and humour. If they finish their work they can do 'nice things'. It is all part of the contract. Sometimes more palpable bribes are tried, using 'chocolate and Smarties and things like that':

> 'The teacher makes it enjoyable because she does it with us on the board quite a lot and I like that because she uses bars of chocolate when we are doing fractions and she cuts it up and shares it between different people, then she gives some away.'　　　(boy, primary)

But for most children the reward is not the 'house points' or the public display. It is the recognition by the teacher of the value of their work:

> 'They know you're trying hard and you've done well.'
>
> (boy, primary)

The 'nice' teacher, then, is not just friendly and consistent. She is also interested in her pupils' work. This is not as obvious as it might appear, for many of the routines of school suggest that tasks have to be done for their own sake and it is hard for the teacher to give individual attention.

The popular teacher displays disinterested concern for all her pupils. Children never convey the impression that general helpfulness, humour and ability to take their needs seriously is a personal matter. In fact they would be embarrassed if the teacher's behaviour were based on anything exclusive to them. The teacher is, after all, 'fair' to all. But teachers also wield power. When children feel a teacher's antipathy rather than liking they feel it personally. The teachers who do not like children are observed to express a dislike towards certain individuals rather than a general hate. Those who are not liked are 'picked on'. Whereas 'niceness' is disinterested, nastiness is personal:

> 'If the teacher speaks to you horribly, then they can't like you.'
>
> (girl, primary)

> 'She sort of picked on me because someone said I was chewing gum in the morning, which I weren't. It was one of my mates it were and I got done for that and now she put me in reading classes.'
>
> (boy, secondary)

It is significant that children really feel they have a close individual connection with a teacher when they are being told off, or are in trouble. At that point, whilst they accept 'strictness' they notice the difference between a general command and an individual emotionally charged 'telling off'. At that point the sense of a comfortable, formal relationship is replaced by an intense *personal* one. This is why they feel 'picked' on:

'If a teacher didn't like you they'd be picking on you all the time and telling you off.'

(boy, primary)

'Once you've done something wrong, they sort of look out for you.'
(boy, secondary)

'Always picking on me, saying it was always me — and if I say I don't, getting me into trouble.'

(boy, secondary)

'Mr G. I'm not very popular with. I was running down the corridor and when I wasn't supposed to and got done for the next day.'
(girl, secondary)

There is a distinction to be made between all the instructions that children are used to obeying or ignoring, which are all part of the background to the classroom, and the pointed reprimand. The latter singles them out. They feel that once they have been noticed it is bound to happen again and again. This sense that it is inevitable that they will be 'picked on' grows in the secondary school. They become more aware of their own reputation just as they become aware of the reputation of teachers. They acquire a growing understanding of the power of gossip. This gives the children a sense of unease about fairness and unfairness:

'I know they're meant to shout at people to get them to do the right thing and that . . . but some people are quiet but the teachers still shout at them, but other people, some people are noisy and the teacher doesn't shout at them so you could get a sign that they liked you.'
(boy, secondary)

'Sometimes they keep picking on you. Say you've been bad in class with your friends. They start shouting at you and send you to different places in the classroom. The teachers that don't like you pick on you.'   (boy, secondary)

Some of the strictures that teachers make seem just; but any punishment is also taken personally, as a sign that there is a sense of animosity on the teacher's behalf, especially towards boys. Children might suggest that rules and discipline are crucial, but they nevertheless feel personally singled out when they receive a punishment. Teachers, with all their power, appear to make arbitrary and immediate judgements and are likely to pick on the wrong person, or the right one for the wrong reasons. So for all the friendliness and help that teachers give, children still remain suspicious of them. There are times when they are not just 'tolerated' for their idiosyncrasies but observed to conduct themselves in a way which is beyond any normal human relationship. Gradually, as children get older, they understand the possibility of having personal friendly relations, often as a result of being taught in smaller groups or sharing the experience of an extra-curricular activity. But for younger children at least, the 'nice' teacher is not a personal friend:

'I would not tell my teacher because she is not part of my home.'
                                                        (girl, primary)

The power of the teacher and the dread of being 'picked on' means that considerable attention is paid to reading signs, to noticing possible changes of mood. Not only language but gestures are scrutinized:

'Well I'm not really sure if the teacher likes me. She looks at me funny.'   (girl, primary)

'I'm not quite sure about Mrs H. because I have got told off quite a few times of her. I think that Mr J. does [like me] because he laughs with me.'   (boy, secondary)

Children are suspicious of teachers when they do not know where they stand with them. Even with those they like and trust there is always the possibility that the teacher might suddenly be harsh and 'pick on' somebody. It is apparent that teachers like some children more than others and treat them according to pre-set judgements rather than to their behaviour at the time:

91

'They'd just treat you kinder than some other people, like if W. was to be in the classroom he'd probably get treated worse than some of the others . . . because he's always being so naughty that no one can trust him now. He's treated OK when he's got a fair chance. It's the way it goes. They just tell him off, start at him, give him detention after school for about ten minutes. Eventually I expect he will learn.'

(girl, secondary)

Nevertheless, with the perceptible shrug of the shoulders such a regime is accepted as necessary, even effective in the long run. Teachers are there to be obeyed, after all, even if they are not fair. Children know the rules and realize that strictness carries the threat of punishment. But even those who are 'picked on' know that there are reasons for this:

'I'm not one of their favourites . . . I'm not naughty but I talk a lot and I don't get on with the work.' (girl, secondary)

The popular teacher is appreciated for being able to listen to and help each child in times of difficulty. The teacher who is feared is not just a stranger but one who seems to take a pleasure in making children aware that they are considered to be silly. Once afraid of the teacher any dialogue is difficult:

'I don't always go to Mrs M. because I'm frightened I look silly to be frightened and worried about work and she might think it's silly to worry about little things.' (girl, primary)

'When I talk with Mrs W. my voice goes all funny. I don't know. My tongue goes all twisted. I get a bit nervous.' (girl, primary)

Some of the most traumatic moments arise when a child behaves as awkwardly as he feels because the teacher induces such nervousness or insecurity that he cannot concentrate in the normal fashion:

'Mrs W. was terrible. She used to take it out on us. I can remember doing a K. and I used to do the big Ks in the infants and I couldn't do the little ks and it took me a long time and then when I was trying to learn something the dinner bell would go and I'd get ever so upset at the dinner break because I though I might get kept in. Once I was trying to read a word and I couldn't find out what this word was and

I went to Miss. It was 'the' and because I couldn't read it I was ever so frightened because she kept going on and on and on.'

(boy, primary)

Some moments are clearly remembered over the years. Just as the 'good' teacher shows patience and humour, the 'bad' teacher makes learning impossible by causing fear and insecurity.

The older children become, the more likely it is that they lose faith in their ability to do good work. By the age of eight children realize some of their academic limitations compared to others, and some begin to give up the struggle to keep up with the work even then. Gradually the answer to failure is to stop trying. The sense of personal discouragement can go very deep. In this context the lack of sustained interest by teachers can be doubly undermining. Teachers are not supposed to be interested in events outside school but are expected to care about the work. When even that does not happen the role of the teacher changes from potential helper to enforcer of authority. Teachers are not always approachable:

'We don't talk much. I don't talk much about my work. I don't talk about anything much to my teacher. I don't feel I could go to any teacher if it was my own problem.'　　　　　(girl, primary)

When teachers do not respond it is the more surprising to children because they see teachers as a central source of information. All the work they do is set, organized and marked by teachers and, in the primary school in particular, almost all the children do revolves around one person. Although they work together in groups, or seek out information from each other and from the library, children know that it is the teacher's central role to *explain*. They recognize that they can turn to the teacher for support when they need it, and do not have to wait for the teacher to approach them. They therefore become used to viewing teachers not as Socratic figures who ask questions and discuss answers, but as people who *know* and are there to respond to their desire for information. The primary teacher is in command of all subjects and is seen as the first and obvious point of enquiry. This view of the teacher's role diminishes somewhat in the secondary school, where the teacher is observed as more authoritarian, more arbitrary and more distant. The sense of trust in the primary school teacher no doubt derives from the amount of time she spends with them and the resulting familiarity, but it is also engendered by the status of the teacher's knowledge:

> 'If I'm worried about work I just go to the teacher and she helps me. If you get it wrong she shows you how to do it . . . and then she makes jokes and tells us how to do it.' (girl, primary)

> 'I'm not worried about asking my teacher about work if I can't do it. She helps me straight away.' (boy, primary)

The important characteristic in the helping teacher is the absence of ridicule or blame if children cannot understand the work they have been asked to do. They are afraid of teachers who think them silly or who make any kind of disparaging remark. The teacher is there to help, not to judge:

> 'If I'm stuck I put my hand up and she comes to my desk and shows me how to do it.' (boy, primary)

> 'I just go to the teacher and ask for help. She tells me what to do, finds an easier way to do the sum.' (girl, primary)

The image of the teacher as a patient, willing source of help and the central source of information is conveyed strongly in the primary school and yet it is the secondary school teacher who is respected for knowledge. It is as if children quickly acquire the general social attitudes towards the growing status of knowledge. This is reflected in contrasts of style. The willing and patient teacher, with concern for each individual's needs, shows attention to learning rather than knowing. The subject specialist is associated with the status of distance, with being busy and unapproachable:

> 'I don't think I'll do that at secondary school because she might be busy and say she can't help.' (boy, primary)

> 'I don't know if I'll be able to go to the comp. teachers. I'll just miss out if I can't understand anything. I wouldn't ask because the teachers are fierce.' (girl, primary)

Children associate a greater level of knowledge with a greater unwillingness to share it. Secondary school teachers are imagined as symbols of erudition and, in primary school children's minds at least, as being the more fierce and distant because of it. Just as the secondary school worries primary children with its aura of power and authority, so do the teachers there:

'I don't think you'll have time to talk to the comp. teacher because you'll be doing work and more work.'   (girl, primary)

'*Here* if you miss anything or don't get it the teacher tells you about it and helps you. You get the chance to do it again. *There* the teachers might tell you "Come on, get on with that work, sit there and be quiet".'   (boy, primary)

The specialist teacher is seen not so much as a source of information but as a setter of work. Friendliness in a teacher is seen as not only extra instruction but a willingness to break away from the routine of work. It is noticeable how the phrase that most characterizes the image of secondary school teachers is the one which marks out a possible interpretation of the limits of their own responsibility — 'Get on with your work.' In the secondary school itself this distance is interpreted as much as a lack of willingness to help in work, and a lack of interest in the personal concerns of children, as unwillingness to be involved if they have any private troubles:

'The teacher hasn't done anything about it.'   (boy, secondary)

'. . . and they just go "go away".'   (girl, secondary)

The secondary teacher's role is far more clearly divided between the pastoral and the academic. The 'delivery' of the curriculum is enough for some teachers. For others 'pastoral' care takes up the whole of their duties. Children's fears of the secondary school teacher is that she will be distant and indifferent and not allow any individual attention, since there will be neither time nor interest. The advantage of having one class teacher for children is that they can be confident that they will not be turned away. Of course such a desire for help depends on the personality of the teacher:

'The teacher is nice and if you had a teacher who was horrible you wouldn't want to get on and learn. It's just because she writes things

95

on the board and that makes it fun because if you had a teacher that just says it out you wouldn't get it all down quickly.' (girl, primary)

'I think it's quite important to know one teacher well. It helps with the teacher, with the teacher's teaching . . . it's talking about what I've got to do. Working out how I should do it and that. I'm not worried about asking my teacher about work if I can't do it. . . . Teachers might not have time to talk at the comp.   (boy, primary)

The good and friendly teacher not only has time to explain things to each individual but can spot when someone needs extra help:

'First I'll try to think it over and read it over and over to see if I've done it before and then Mrs ____ might see me thinking and ask me out to see what's the matter.'   (boy, primary)

Despite their fears, children in secondary school find it possible to have close relations with teachers. In the absence of the domination of one class teacher, the sense of the really personal and individual contact can be taken further:

'Well, the staff here tend to talk a lot more and are very talkative to you whereas back there they would be talking to you in the whole group and not usually as one person quite often.'   (boy, secondary)

The teacher as a source of information in the primary school is approached as if a fount of all wisdom. But the very generality of response to all the children in the classroom on a variety of topics and in a variety of ways suggests that there is less expectation of any intense individual sharing of knowledge. The primary classroom, with its holistic curriculum, is a collective enterprise. Once the rules are established the classroom imposes its own routines, but such a shared sense of purpose is only brought about by the teacher's imposition of rules. Whether the teachers are there to support pastoral needs or to deliver the curriculum, they also acknowledge that their centrality lies in their control.

Children accept that teaching includes the keeping of discipline. Conveying information is part of status and authority. Teachers are expected to be strict, and children resent those who cannot impose order:

'Mr ____ tends to let people muck around. It's like he's deaf or blind because everyone's playing around during class and not getting on.'

(boy, secondary)

But at the same time children resent interference by teachers when they think it unjustified. 'Strictness' can be defined not as a determination to keep order but as a constant bullying presence, a nagging interest in work not being done well:

'I don't like teachers who are strict. You're sometimes just writing something and you're there trying to figure it out and they want to know what you're doing and you say "I'm trying to figure out what to do" and they say "Get on, don't sit there, come and see me."'

(boy, primary)

The teacher needs to keep a balance between explanation and interference. Perhaps the distinction is that of tone: how to convey a genuine interest in the work of the class and the individual, or how to convey pre-set standards against which to measure the children's success or, more significantly, failure. Children appreciate encouragement and resent being constantly told off. They expect teachers to have high standards, but they do not expect a constant stream of blame for failure to meet those standards. They praise clarity but dislike the shift from instruction to punishment. For a number of children the strictness of teachers can be overdone, a harshness for its own sake rather than for the sake of teaching:

'If Miss _____ come in we know if we don't pay attention for one minute she'll snap our heads off, so it calms me down if I read.'

(girl, primary)

Certain kinds of pressure seem to have the opposite effect from that intended, driving children into fear and a lack of confidence in themselves. The lack of 'explanation' is transferred into harassment:

'At primary you used to be able to talk quietly or something. You came into the classroom and you're all talking quietly and now you're not allowed to talk at all or he says "shut up."' (boy, secondary)

The teacher's voice echoes in a series of instructions:

'Don't touch things until the teacher tells you, in metalwork, and don't sit down until they tell you and don't get the things out until you're asked.' (boy, secondary)

It all seems to depend on whether all the teacher has to say is interpreted constructively or negatively. The instructions can make things happen, and help children understand. Conversely, the teacher's voice can be associated primarily with prevention, with punishment and blame. There are, after all, traditional methods of teaching that have nothing to do with encouragement:

> 'When Mr ____ does the tests at school if we don't get eight we have to stay in and learn the words and when we've learned the words we can go out. It's a spelling test. It's pretty frightening.'
>
> (girl, primary)

Some of the work given to children becomes the stuff of punishment, or the excuse for punishment:

> 'Sometimes they take the book off you ... if you talk while the teacher's talking you get sent to a corner and do different work.'
>
> (boy, primary)

> '... and when you show Mrs ____ your work you just get told off.'
>
> (girl, primary)

Lack of order and the misuse of punishments is resented, not because children resent rules, discipline or strictness, but because the failure to create the right working atmosphere is a sign of failure in a teacher. The 'good teacher', after all is strict:

> 'With a good teacher you can get on better, but with a soft teacher you can't do much.' (girl, secondary)

Over-strictness, or the giving out of punishments, is never considered good teaching, for it looks like an unnecesary loss of control:

> 'Well, they're all right as people but they shout and don't keep good order, and you can't work in their class. I feel bad when teachers shout ____ they shouldn't shout. [Good teachers] keep order by the way they teach. They don't need to shout. It's not like they never shout. Sometimes if a person need a shock you need to shout, but mostly no.' (boy, secondary)

The balance between strictness and harshness is obviously a delicate one. Children appreciate the teacher who is firm but approachable, who makes absolutely clear what her expectations are and yet has enough flexibility to respond to different people and different circumstances. Over-firmness is considered a failure, a sign of inadequacy, as much as over-indulgence. The desire to be feared undermines a teacher as much as a desire to be liked. But whilst children make the teacher the anchor on which all other things depend, trusting in stability, and whilst children want to know where they stand in relation to the firm ground, they do not expect rigidity and inflexibility. Changeability is a fault when it comes to control, but adaptability and variety are virtues when it comes to passing on knowledge.

Children seek a mixture of activities in learning. They like to do safe, secure, well-known tasks, but they also wish to be challenged by different teaching methods. This tension between excitement and the everyday, between new challenges and the knowledge of what is familiar is an important matter for children. They mention it when talking about the curriculum, and they mention it when they talk about teachers. Their discussion of various teaching styles make it plain that they expect both a consistency of approach so that they know where they are, and a flexibility, a touch of the unexpected, to keep them interested. Too many changes, or a lack of clear explanation, like inconsistencies in terms of discipline, make them feel worried, and worried in such a way that they tend to take it out on themselves, to become disillusioned with their own work so that they no longer expect anything from themselves. Too much 'consistency', the familiar routine, the absolute certainty of knowing what to do that comes of repetition, makes them feel that their work does not matter. Experiences they call 'boring' are those things which either do not stretch them at all or which try to stretch them too much.

To get the balance right is clearly difficult:

'Sometimes I'm not sure what they're talking about.'

(girl, secondary)

'They explain something really easy and then they say "Do you understand?", and they explain it again, but you've understood it the first time.'

(boy, secondary)

The teaching style children admire is one in which individual attention and individual demands are balanced against the needs of the class as a whole. Children seem to understand the difficulties for the teacher and do not demand too much time spent on themselves rather than on the whole class. But they do expect *some* personal knowledge and awareness of their own difficulties. Things that remain unexplained become resented. They resent being given work that is presented merely to keep them occupied. When they observe various teaching styles, therefore, they make it clear that the ideal is one in which all the various factors, between the individual and the group, the demands of the subject and the clarity of the explanation, are carefully balanced. Although they rarely talk to each other about the perfect teacher or the perfect lesson (as opposed to unpopular teachers), children convey a clear picture of the relationship with the teacher that they would like, and the way in which they would like teachers to perform. They can judge the style of teaching separately from the character of the teacher, although the two overlap, and they are clear about which factors make for a poor teaching style.

Teaching is not a single activity, nor do most teachers rely on one method of conveying information, or one way of controlling the class.[5] Children observe and emulate a variety of activities, for the classroom is a complex place:

'Some of the time we do them out of primary maths books, sometimes we do it off a sheet and on the board with the teacher or like when you have a test to know your ability in maths. We do games in maths. The Fletcher books are the best. We go outside measuring. We measured the playground, and we measured the music room. We do quite a lot of work like that. We do tables. Miss shouts them out and we put our hands up and answer them. They've got different ways of teaching. . . .'   (girl, primary)

Many of the tasks are familiar and would seem to be routines, but children show an awareness of a number of different activities that make lessons interesting. They are accustomed to responding to a wide range of instructions, but they also appreciate the teacher's attempts to give them a variety of tasks. They wish to *do* things, to be involved in discovering information, in seeing things happen. They like subjects that demand such involvement:

'Learning your tables isn't fun but *doing* things is.'   (boy, primary)

'It's very enjoyable because in the English lessons the teacher adds things into it and in the maths, pictures and that and puzzles in maths that you have to work out, games and things and that's nicer than just having a page out of your key maths to do.'   (girl, primary)

The desire for variety, however, is not just a matter of wanting to be entertained. The teacher is understood to try different approaches as a means of conveying understanding. Children acknowledge the complexity of a teacher's task, and realize that teachers are trying to find ways of helping them understand. Children do not assume that the teacher merely 'delivers' the curriculum. On the contrary, they respect and respond to any attempt to clarify through activity. Variety in teaching is not seen as a distraction, a waste of time, or as a lack of intellectual demand. It is seen to be at the service of learning.

The more time children have to observe the teacher, as in primary school, the more will they expect a variety of teaching methods. The holistic nature of primary practice partly accounts for this, but the result is a suspicion of the picture of the traditional teacher as depicted in secondary schools:

'I think they [secondary school teachers] will expect you to understand it without doing things . . . I think they'll tell us what to do. They'll say things like $\frac{5}{12}$ of etc. and we'll have to do it in our books. They'll just say it or write it on the board. They won't do diagrams or anything like that.'   (girl, primary)

Children see the games and activities that teachers give them as a means of learning. To them such tasks are the other side of explanations; ideas made clear through action. Their enthusiasm for different teaching techniques is in contrast to the suspicion their parents have for what the latter think of as games. Children see the connection between learning and activity; their parents tend to remain suspicious of 'modern' teaching methods. For the children the teacher's ability to explain will result in a variety of tasks, all of which are seen to be conducive to learning. For this reason it is important for children to know *what* they are learning through their activities.

It is also important for children to know that all that teachers do is consistent with their need to learn, and sensitive to individual children's needs. Children are bewildered by changing styles, by contrasting types of presentation and expectation. When teachers are inconsistent in their styles and demands, children are nonplussed. When the style changes between schools or between teachers, the result is a worrying lack of clarity:

> 'I do the maths half the way I learn in Cheshire and half the way I do it here so I kept on getting it wrong because I was doing a bit of both and I didn't realize it. So I hope they'll teach me the way I know at the comp. because now I'm beginning to do it the way I've learned it here and to change back again I'd get muddled up and that worries me.'
> (boy, primary)

> 'If our teacher's away another teacher comes in and says you don't do it that way, you do it a different way, you've been doing it wrong. The teachers might think you're no good at work if you're untidy.'
> (girl, primary)

> 'I didn't particularly like it with the students when we were doing topics. Because you did things one way and she did some things the opposite.'
> (boy, primary)

Consistency in teaching style, and in children's understanding of what they are supposed to do, is crucial. Provided that children know what they are expected to do, and are encouraged, it does not seem so important which particular style is adopted. The security of knowing what method to use is at the heart of children's feelings of success in learning.

The delicate matter of striking a balance between variety and consistency reveals something about the difficulties of the teacher's task. Children do not expect any rigid routine, but assume that all they are asked to do makes sense. They appear to be after an inner sense of purpose in learning, a purpose that is clear in many different kinds of task. For this reason children expect teachers to remain consistently themselves, and yet able to respond to demands outside the classroom, to take on a pastoral as well as an academic role. Children do not wish the relationship with teachers to be eternally formal. They look forward to the possibility of having some friendly gesture outside the confines of the classroom:

'Like at dinner times when she sits on our table, we have a good chat then. She talks to the whole class in the classroom. She talks to me when she's taking lessons separately on your own.' (boy, primary)

'We always have a chat. Not just me but all the class.'

(girl, primary)

The general cohesion of the primary class is also perceived as giving opportunities for a variety of types of relationship, and contrasts with what children experience as the fleeting formality of the many teachers in the secondary school.

The qualities of humour, responsiveness, firmness and the ability to present a variety of interesting tasks are all perceived by children as being the mark of the good teacher. But if there is one overriding concern amongst all children, it is that teachers should take the time and trouble to *explain*. It is the one word that all children use to describe what they hope for — "She shows you clearly what to do, and will explain things." They find no work too difficult if it is explained to them, even if it means that the teacher comes back to it again and again — "the next year she'll do it again, so we can understand more". Children do not imply that certain things are impossible to understand. The difficulties they have derived not from the material itself, but the way it is presented to them. One dimension to understanding is time:

'In Scotland, see, we only went through learning for about five minutes, then we had to sit down again and get on with it. I find it better to go through it for a bit longer before you sit down and write it. Otherwise you do it wrong and it has to be done all over again. It's wasting time and you think you don't understand what you're doing.'

(girl, primary)

Children expect teachers to be able to explain lucidly. Failure to communicate can be the result of inappropriate demands, or muddle or indifference. It is not important to children if the teacher chooses to try to explain a point to an individual or to the whole class, as long as she tries to explain. The 'good' teacher is responsive to groups and individuals:

'I like more explaining. More samples. I get stuck and muddled. Then I try to work it out and if I can't I go to Mrs _____ then she helps me and I find out the rest by myself.' (girl, primary)

'I put my hand up and ask when I can't understand. The teacher helps me. If I can't still get it I stay in at break and stand at Miss's desk and she can help me. Then I understand it a lot better. I get fed up trying to work things out. If I get stuck at the comp. I'll ask my dad.'   (boy, primary)

'If you still don't understand you can go up to her and she explains it. Like fractions or anything you don't understand. Now I do because she does them again with you and shows you.'   (girl, primary)

The primary classroom is full of the possibility of individual attention, which takes time. Although we know that it is difficult for teachers to give such attention to all the members of the class, children nevertheless relish the opportunity.[6] They also assume that the secondary school will not give them the chance to be treated as an individual:

'Well, the teacher at the comp. might say, "Well, you've heard me. Think it out for yourself. Sit down and carry on."'   (girl, primary)

Primary children value the teacher as a source of information, and as someone willing to help, not so much as an easy way out of having to think for themselves but as the best means of learning. Their fear of the secondary school is that the teachers will no longer explain; that the work will be delivered and pupils left to get on with it:

'They probably won't write anything on the board when you're learning maths. They'll just tell you. Or they might not even tell you. They'll tell you to turn to a page when it just says at the top and you'll have to find it from the book.'   (boy, primary)

Secondary school children find some of their fears corroborated by experience. They also criticize the indifference that is manifested in the lack of individual attention:

'I don't think it's explained really well. She's writing letters or something — and she just says "Get on with the piece of work you were doing last week!" But if you've been away and you don't know what to do you go up to her and she says "No, go and sit down", and you just have to do what everyone else is doing. She never talks to us. She's always writing.'   (girl, secondary)

Balancing the individual's needs with the needs of the class as a whole is a complex demand on the role of the teacher. Children notice, and approve of those who manage to strike the right note by using a variety of classroom strategies. The teacher who is appreciated provides different activities and demonstrates knowledge of the children that is based on diagnosis and explanation:

> 'Well, she teaches the whole group and then she tells you on your own. She does work on the board. We use wheels and things . . . if you don't understand it you can go to the teacher and talk about it. If you're just lazy she'll tell you off.' (girl, primary)

Children recognize that explanations can be as much use when given to the whole group as when delivered to the individual. But they also know that useful instructions are directed at their understanding, implying the teacher *knows* them well enough to be aware of what is going wrong:

> 'When we are finding it difficult she talks a lot to the whole class. She doesn't always talk to one person, just when they go up. If about eight people keep doing it wrong she talks to the whole classroom.'
> (boy, primary)

Children do not expect the teacher to spend all their time either dealing with the presentation of new facts, or to be responsive only to their individual needs:

> 'Instead of standing round the desk all the time and wasting time he reads out the answers. For marking. He gives us nice worksheets instead of using books all the time. He makes them up himself and that makes them better to do. He kind of puts them in his own words. It's easier as well.' (boy, secondary)

The variety children seek is expressed in the balance between individual and group activities and by the teacher's ability to 'translate' the dry materials into something interesting.

In the eyes of primary school children the concept of the permanent class and the same teacher implies an interest in their individual work and the ability to explain. Such explanation takes place as much in group activities as with individuals. Children say that they *like* to be together, in some kind of collective:

'I prefer doing it with all the class than just set from a book. The teacher does it on the board and writes things and everybody gets a chance to answer them. So it's not like in a book when you're the only one who can try to answer them. Everybody can do it and I like that better.'   (girl, primary)

'If we're starting something new, like fractions, she tells the whole class. If the person who's doing has finished she tells another one.'
(boy, primary)

When primary school children talk about the 'whole class' they imply a mixture of group and individual work. In the secondary school one or two of the assumptions that were made earlier about teachers are confirmed:

'The teachers stand up and tell you what was. After, she sat down and she said "You can all get on with it now."'   (boy, secondary)

At the same time the memories of primary school teaching change. The sense of the individual teacher's explanations is lost, and the distance of instruction recalled. The greater the interval between the experience and the memory of it, the more formal and less effective it seems:

'At my other school they didn't do much board teaching. They just sat you down with a book and told you to do it and at this school they explain it first and then you have to do it.'   (girl, secondary)

Children defend whatever school they are in and tend to be suspicious of the other. But on teaching styles they are all agreed. They admire the ability to explain. They dislike being told to 'get on with it', and not knowing what they are supposed to do. Children most fear the kind of presentation that assumes that they will know automatically what they are supposed to do. They fear that their needs will not be recognized, and they cannot tell if other children feel the same:

'I think that teachers just say what we are going to do and just kind of get on and do it.'   (girl, primary)

'They'll just give you something to do, even if you don't know. They don't explain it to you at first.'   (boy, primary)

Children project on to the secondary school all those fears that

106

are their worst experiences at primary school. They fear the association of learning with blame, failure, with dread of what is to come, whether of the test or the punishment. Children all appreciate the teacher who explains *before* they do their work, rather than waiting for them to flounder. They are aware of the fact that there is so much that they cannot understand and that there is a lot to be learned, but they also wish to be *taught*.

In some cases children become accustomed to a routine in which they are expected to get on with work and know what the work is: 'You were just told what you had to do and got on with it.' In some cases the 'routine' means that the teacher remains 'safe' behind the desk. But children adapt to that if they know what they are expected to do:

'You just go straight into it and start work. You know where everything is.' (girl, secondary)

Secondary schools after all do not need such variety *within* lessons. Instead the moves from one area of the curriculum to another provide their own form of variety and routine:

'Well, in between every lesson you know what you're doing next and you go to different teachers all the time and you move about. You always know what you're going to do next and I like that.'

(boy, secondary)

It does not need a flamboyant teacher to make it clear to the class what is expected of them:

'You come into your own classroom. There's a teacher sitting there waiting for you. Then you go out and come in and she's there sitting down waiting for you, and you get on with your work 'cos you know what she wants you to do.' (girl, secondary)

Provided expectations are clear, even the ability to provide a variety of experiences becomes less urgent. The knowledge of the teacher's expectations in the work of the primary school classroom is continued, even with difficulty, into the secondary schools. In either case the children desire the security of knowing the teacher's expectations, and of being encouraged.

The ways in which children view teachers are not surprising when they are tested against the evidence of observation and experience. But their significance is rarely taken into account, for so much more could be achieved by following rules of consistency, variety and explanation. The effects of a teacher who is not in real control of herself or her teaching can be traumatic. The sense of dread can pervade children's approach to their work, and undermine their progress for years. And yet, although teachers wield great power, children remain objective and even laconically ironic about their performance. They know that there are times when teachers are justified in shouting, but they also know that shouting can be a sign of failure. They know the distinction between those who choose when to reveal the authority of their will and those who need to assert themselves to overcome their lack of authority. Some teachers use discipline as a form of social control; others appear to do so out of lack of self-control. There are occasions when particular teachers are unfair, arbitrary in their judgements and driven by moods.

The symptoms of failure in teachers can be summed up in a case study of a teacher in a secondary school. This is the case of one who, in his own eyes, might be deliberately creating a rule of law, but who in the eyes of children is to be feared and resented for his lack of consistency. This teacher, 'Mr T.', symbolizes many of the facets that children dislike. He attacks their work and makes them feel it is worthless. He creates tension so that they find it hard to work. He is arbitrary in his judgements and his shouting seems out of control. He picks on individuals with such bewildering rapidity that they have no idea who will be his next victim, or why. And at the same time he is seen to be a 'creep', to want to be liked or at least justified in his behaviour. Children assume that this is in case the other teachers hear of their complaints.

Mr T. is equally fierce to boys and girls, but the boys take it far more laconically since they are far more accustomed to such attacks. To them Mr T. is just an extreme example of what is accepted as their lot — 'he just goes nutty' (boy). 'He shouts and has a go at you. I don't take much notice' (boy). But all find working in such an atmosphere difficult: to some it matters more. Mr T. makes a point of damaging children's esteem of their own work:

'It upsets me when he shouts. He shouted at me once and I felt upset. He said my work was rubbish.' (girl)

'He starts telling people that they're not very clever, and their work isn't good and all that.' (girl)

Such an attitude towards the work is part of a more general attitude towards the children as a whole, an attitude that is an almost deliberate creation of tension. The children do not know where they stand:

'First time I went there, he said to everyone, "Stand up," and we did — then the others sat down and I was still standing up. I got all told off, and he started getting his ruler out and hitting you on the knuckles and that — and he goes bright red when he tells you off, and you try not to laugh, and he goes calm and then he suddenly starts shouting at you. So we don't talk at all, we just get on with our work, not even looking around.' (girl)

'Mr T. does get angry if we ask after he's explained something — he's often in a bad mood.' (boy)

'I get kind of very nervous and when he shouts I'm sort of edgy and then I make mistakes . . . he says its 'cos of us that he shouts, but I don't think it is really.' (girl)

Children detect in Mr T. a lack of control over himself rather than the use of tension to create a working atmosphere. Up to a point one could assume that he is just a fierce disciplinarian who uses all the most obvious weapons of a powerful teacher over children, as if these were a necessary response to their natural depravity. But children accept normal discipline that is a response to their misbehaviour and their tendency to misbehave. They find that Mr T.'s shouting is something else:

'Mr T. shouts a bit when he gets angry — he really does shout. Once he got really angry with us — I don't know why — and he said "Whenever your class comes in, it always makes me angry" — we didn't know why he said that.' (girl)

'Anything we do — every peek — he shouts at another person that's right near you — it can be . . . well, I know I'm a bit silly now . . . but a bit scared. You dunno what he's going to do, turn . . . I put me head down and prayed.' (boy)

'Yes, but they don't go bright red and shout at everybody. He's shouted at me twice.' (girl)

The sense that children are left with is of a teacher who 'picks on' anyone, but who makes each person 'picked on' feel that it is both personal and arbitrary:

'I don't like Mr T. 'cos he's always picking on other children in our class, and it's not fair on them, and you never know who he's going to pick on next. He did it to my friend Michelle the other day and she burst out crying 'cos she did her best, it took her half an hour to do her story the other day and then Mr T. he said that it really was horrible and she might have to do it again and she burst out crying, and then in the end he tried to be all nice to her and as if he hadn't done it. I think he was trying to stop her from telling people so that he won't be a teacher who was disliked by every other teacher. He said to Michelle when he was trying to be nice that he couldn't help it — couldn't help being nasty to people. . . . He finds different people. First he picked on Deena and then there's two boys who sit together. He's always picking on them, and there was one boy called Gary and he made him move and he didn't even do anything — I don't know what he did — I think he dropped his pen and went to pick it up. Who's he going to start on next? I try my best to do my homework — I try to calm myself down in the lesson and half-way through he starts shouting, and goes all red and he shouts at someone and your heart sort of jumps.' (girl)

Such a series of observations of the mixture of personal attacks, apologies and uncontrolled temper is not unique:

'Well, he screams at you — he doesn't just shout "Don't do it" — he screams at you, and like afterwards, one of my friends got really upset 'cos he had a go at her about her work in front of the whole class, which I don't think's fair, and he kept me back 'cos I sit next to her, and we're friends and he started, like, being more friendly, and saying "I'm your friend". I don't think that's right — you go crawling back to a child after you've started at them just to become their friends.' (girl)

Mr T. reveals two characteristics of the closely observed teacher's failure. He is, firstly, inconsistent. It would be preferable for children if he were over-strict, for at least that would be a particular professional style. The children are fearful of his arbitrariness, of his changes of mood and the way in which he might pick on any of them at any time. They take every generalized onslaught personally. In Mr T.'s case it *is* a personal matter. For his second characteristic is that he reveals himself. He is not just fulfilling the duties of a teacher, acting with the authority of the professional. He is being driven by uncontrolled personal feelings, by his own insecurities and inadequacies. His inconsistency lies not just in the changes of tone but in the exaggerations of them. When he is not shouting he is trying to be a friend — 'crawling' for pity. Children observe the disturbed personality, and despise it.

Children observe the tensions between the personality of the teacher and the role she has to play. They accept the need for the teacher to keep discipline, and yet appreciate a teacher who can do it well enough to allow for humour and approachability. The effective explanations of teachers are those which are in a calm and structured context. In a sense, Mr T. exaggerates all the characteristics of the teacher; he is the symbol of the balance between the public and the private gone wildly out of control. But the teacher as an individual always needs to be in harmony with the teacher as a member of an institution, as someone symbolizing authority.

The role of teachers in their relationship with children is a condition of their position as members of an institution. The children's sense of each adult's personal characteristics is subsumed, within the school, by a view of teachers as people who are given and promote a collective authority and who are not just individuals but part of a corporate whole. There can be nothing quite like the role of the teacher in the school. Other professionals have their own power and authority, but no others are quite so dependent on the power that derives from an institution and the need to impose this power collectively. The doctor, for example, can hide behind the obscurities and aura of professional expertise. People approach the doctor, individually, for help and advice. Teachers, however, must impose their authority and their professional expertise on groups of children, whether they like it or not. Whilst schools are sometimes seen as a microcosm of society, there is no other job quite like that of the teacher, and this is naturally felt by the children.

Children see their teachers as demonstrations of the corporate life of the school, and as experts within their own authority. They also understand them and react to them as individual human

111

beings, with their own idiosyncrasies, strengths and weaknesses. Children understand how much depends on the way in which a teacher will create and establish a particular relationship with a class. They also understand that this is not just a matter of the professional competence of the teacher, but of her personal characteristics, confidence, determination and subtlety. In whatever ways the power that teachers use is defined, the role that they adopt is the outcome of their position as members of a school.

By virtue of their role in the school, teachers have the potential for charismatic qualities, even if only some of them achieve them fully. Weber defines charisma as a quality of the individual which sets him apart from ordinary men.[7] Even if his interest lies in those with almost superhuman qualities, he makes it clear that such a position of leadership and inaccessibility could also be applied to teachers. Charisma, after all, implies some kind of authority.[8] The sense of separateness and the specific definition of a particular role are important.[9] The position as representative of an institutional structure seems equally essential.[10] But all these definitions of charisma explore the more public domains in which a large part of a population can be swayed by the public statements of particular men. In the classroom, every day, there is such a potential of the use of personality to influence and cajole the minds of children. This is why every teacher has at least the potential to be a charismatic figure.

But children are not usually so caught up in the personality of the teacher that she could be defined as 'charismatic'. From their comments it is clear that the position of authority and distance is only one side of charisma. Children wish to respect their teachers, to know where they are with them. They wish to see them being strict, conveying their authority and holding to themselves a sense of public rectitude that gives no one in the class the chance to undermine authority. At the same time children wish to be liked, to receive individual attention and to feel that they can both trust and understand what the teacher is saying. The children make a distinction between the quality of caring, especially for the slower learners, and the quality of teaching.[11] They note, separately, those skills of making a subject understandable and the willingness to respond to individual difficulties. They also assume that the more distant teachers in secondary schools will be 'better' even if they cannot follow what they are saying. The charisma of the individual teacher is a combination of the authority that derives from a professional role and the perceivable interest in the lives of children, showing a willingness to share jokes and interests. Distance is not enough by itself. Friendliness is not always respected.

That balance between friendliness and distance which distinguishes charisma also characterizes the equivocal way in which children look at teachers. The role of the teacher contains all the elements that make charisma possible; a position of power and authority and the need to win the approval of the pupils in her charge. All teachers, therefore, find themselves in a rather special position. Some element of charisma affects all teachers, but the amount varies a great deal. Children soon indicate their opinions to each other, having instinctively recognized those teachers who go too far in one direction or the other; those who are too distant and those who are not distant enough. At the same time children's attitudes towards teachers contain both recognition of their importance and an underlying suspicion of their motives and power. The need for the good teacher, the one who makes lessons lively and takes an interest in individual children without breaking the formal boundary of control, is felt strongly by children who wish to have things 'explained'. At the same time relatively few teachers fulfil this need.

In the primary school, with few teachers to compare, children are tolerant and able to judge that the class teacher, whom they study at length, actually does care and does her best. In secondary schools comparisons are easier to make, and the variety of teaching styles they meet means that the children are constantly testing the teacher, finding out how each one will react to pressure. Nevertheless, children often indicate their toleration of teachers. They put up with their little whims, their tantrums and the general level of rudeness that characterizes classroom dialogue. Teachers are a subject of very close study, since so much depends on them. Pupils' sense of tolerance comes about because they are observing not only how the teacher controls the class, and maintains authority, but also how well the teacher communicates what is being taught. But the emotional energy is directed not at the teacher as a role so much as the teacher as a personality. Pupils observe what pleases the teacher, and what the teacher expects of them. They also observe what makes teachers lose their self-command and learn how to change their teachers' minds.

Children spend much time judging the mood of the teacher; seeing how far they can go before the teacher reacts. Their awareness of emotional nuance is subtle. Just as they reflect each other's moods so they discriminate between the teacher's 'good' days and 'bad' days, knowing *when* they can approach the teacher with temerity. Children's emotional sense of teachers is constantly alert. Their intellectual sense of what the teacher wants is also under constant review. Although teachers know that there are great differences between 'open' and 'closed' questions, those to which there could be any number of individual responses, and those to which there is only one factual answer, to children *all* questions are closed.[12] As much intellectual attention is paid to guessing what the teacher *wants* as to thinking about the answer. The authority of the teacher as well as the dominance of her role derives from this constant guesswork, the close attention to everything they do. Teachers therefore dominate the emotional life of the classroom in a way which is unlike any other circumstances that children subsequently meet. Knowing this, children combine a laconic forgiveness for human weakness, a high expectation of professional behaviour and a fascination with the teacher's performance:

> 'You don't get cross when they don't understand but you do get cross when they don't listen.'　　　　　　　　　　　　　(boy, primary)

NOTES AND REFERENCES

1. Mortimore, P., Sammons, P., Stoll, L., Lewis, D. and Ecob, R. *School Matters: The Junior Years*. London: Open Books, 1988. Rutter, M., Maughan, B., Mortimore, P. and Ouston, J. *Fifteen Thousand Hours — Secondary Schools and Their Effects on Children*. London: Open Books, 1979.
2. Sharp, R. and Green, A. *Education and Social Control: A Study in Progressive Primary Education*. London: Routledge and Kegan Paul, 1975.
3. King, R., *All Things Bright and Beautiful? A Sociological Study of Infants' Classrooms*. Chichester: Wiley, 1978.

4. Measor, L., and Woods, P. *Changing Schools: Pupil Perspectives on Transfer to a Comprehensive.* Milton Keynes: Open University Press, 1984.

5. Galton, M., Simon, B. and Croll, P. *Inside a Primary Classroom.* London: Routledge and Kegan Paul, 1980.

6. When researchers such as the Oracle team, or Bennett and Desforges, try to measure the amount of time given to individual interactions between pupil and teacher, they find it is very limited, perhaps a few minutes per week.

7. Weber, M. *The Theory of Social and Economic Organisation.* New York: Oxford University Press, 1947. pp. 358–359.

8. Stills, E. 'Charisma, order, status.' *American Sociological Review* **30,** 199–213, 1965.

9. Spencer, M. 'What is charisma?' *British Journal of Sociology* **24** (3), 345–350, 1973.

10. Asch, S. 'Forming impressions of personality.' *Journal of Abnormal and Social Psychology* **41,** 258–290, 1946.

11. Mitman, A. 'Teachers' differential behaviour towards higher and lower achieving students and its relation to selected teacher characteristics.' *Journal of Educational Psychology* **77** (2), 149–161, 1985.

12. See Barnes, D. *Language and Learning in Secondary Schools.* Harmondsworth: Penguin, 1965. A typical 'closed' question is 'What is a watershed?'

CHAPTER 8
The Experience of Learning

'The subjects are all right. I just don't get along with the teachers.'
(boy, secondary)

Teachers are dominating influences on the experiences of school. But they are not the whole experience. Nearly all social aspects of school, from individual friendships to larger groups, are defined against, or in spite of, teachers. The private everyday experience of school includes awareness of teachers, but it is not really entered by teachers. Even formal aspects of learning remain a private experience, one of individual struggle and personal meaning in which other people, teachers or friends, only impinge at times. As in the assembly where the individual child is aware of the teacher's expectations, yet thinking his own thoughts, responding to secret whispers but also making his own observations, the actual experience of learning is complex. It is also an experience which is unstructured and unplanned, individual not only by necessity but by default.

Learning can never be wholly planned. Chance associations or insights play as significant a role as assiduous accumulation of knowledge. Even teachers, for all their detailed planning, have to adapt to how the class responds, to interruptions and to the opportunities that present themselves in the dynamics of the classroom. Children's actual learning is not only unplanned but a matter of chance, and rarely fully aware. They are presented with tasks to fulfil and copy out of school-books or do routine mathematics, but this is not the same as learning. They seek to give what the teacher wants of them, or to remain obscurely out of sight, and pass the time. Even when children are spending their day 'on task', the outward semblance of concentration can cover up private thoughts and private messages, day-dreams and speculations on quite different topics. Much of the time is spent with a book to write in and a ready pen. But notice how little is written, and how rarely the pen is used.

Children's judgements of what teachers require show sophistication in the art of avoiding work. Mostly this sophistication is rewarded, for each is one amongst many and the classroom is an environment rich in camouflage. The girl quietly making no fuss in her corner whilst the boys are causing a nuisance is just as clever at avoiding learning. But all children want to remain invisible, unnoticed. For their experience is always private. They do not want to be cajoled into learning. They have the general human tendency to be suspicious of being taught. And when they are learning they know that it is their own. Their ownership of learning makes it real, and private.

When children have a distinct task and are engaged upon it they might work slowly or not at all. Sometimes they are undergoing routines, or just passing time.[1] But one of their significant experiences of both primary and secondary school ostensibly has little to do with any formal learning, and yet it is an extension of children's actual experience of school. It is the amount of time spent waiting. Children wait in the corridor until they are allowed into the classroom, they wait for the teacher to begin, until everyone is quiet, they wait for the signal that tells them to change what they are doing, and wait in the hall or the playground for the bell. Of course they fill these gaps, with talking, dreaming or playing; and they become accustomed to spending time. But it is waiting, nevertheless, filling an empty space.

Children are not slow workers. But the amount of work produced in a given time is often remarkably small. They are passing the time. Even when engaged in a task, children are finding means to postpone the action. They require a pen. They need fresh paper. Their neighbour has an idea. The teacher is telling someone off. The sun is warm in the window. Attempts to measure the amount of time the children spend waiting, in the classroom and outside, waiting to start work or pretending to do it, might face the difficulties of precise measurement, or the peculiar circumstances of that classroom. But they rarely suggest that less than two-thirds of children's time is spent 'waiting'.[2] Children accept this as part of their normal school experience.

The wadding of routine surrounds the highlights of memorable experiences. It is like a context that makes sense of the rest, and also explains the paucity of memories from such a rich experience. For school is a routine, one imposed by the timetable and another by the teacher. Some routines are structural, so that children associate boredom in school with 'writing', being occupied. Others are clearly a part of the general, slow, organization of the school, like moving from topic to topic or classroom to classroom.

In such a context children ache for variety. They yearn for different styles of working, for experiments in science, for something that fires them and the teacher. They look forward to those moments when the sharing of excitement replaces the routines, when they are learning something that even interests the teacher rather than something that keeps them occupied. In this context children appreciate changes in routine:

> 'I think it is very good in the primary school the way you have to do everything in the same day, like a bit of reading and a bit of topics and a bit of maths every day.'   (boy, primary)

Even if the style of learning might seem the same, different topics suggest different kinds of presentation, so that children notice what is going on rather than taking it for granted. But such changes of routine are in the hands of the teacher. The primary school has both the advantage and disadvantage of having the opportunity to create variety, and time. Looking back on their experiences, secondary children sense the peace of a place in which they were not constantly being rushed off to learn something new:

> 'You had time to finish your work there. You haven't got it here.'
> (girl, secondary)

> '. . . and they've got a certain amount of time but lessons at primary school just went on and on until the teacher decided to change to another.'   (boy, secondary)

The daily routine and the gaps between different tasks are created largely by the class teacher in the primary school, but by the timetable in the secondary school. Variety is imposed:

> 'You'll have to write out a timetable to know where you've got to go to next.'   (boy, primary)

In either case waiting is a significant part of the experience:

'. . . because most of the time they've nothing to do at the comp. You just wander about anyway. So really you might as well finish up all your work and then go home.' (girl, secondary)

The traditional role of the class teacher in the primary school centres on different uses of time and a different style of work from that of the secondary school.[3] But waiting is implicit in both kinds of system, whether the substantial amounts of waiting take place within or between lessons. Children do not always find time spent in a desultory way pleasurable or stimulating. They stress the fact that much of the school's routine and much of their experience of learning is boring. They find many of the tasks they are set boring, and they all find particular subjects boring. In fact they accept that school will inevitably contain boring moments. They associate many activities with boredom. And although they find ways of mitigating their boredom, they accept it as an essential attribute of school. The question remains whether such a widespread view is inevitable.

Children find particular kinds of work, like writing, particularly boring. They find many tasks that are presented to them a kind of mechanical routine:

'You get these books, right, and there's a sheet with all the questions on, and you've got to find the questions in the books. It's boring. Finding the answers is boring.' (girl, primary)

A study of some of the textbooks on mathematics or 'comprehension' shows how mechanical and repetitive many of the exercises are. It is as if they had no particular purpose beyond keeping the children occupied. Children are quick to detect those times when routine sets in and the teacher tells them to 'get on' with something. They are also quick to notice when teachers are not efficient in their presentation of materials:

'I got a bit bored because when we were making remote-controlled buggies he went on and on and we never got a chance to make them.' (girl, secondary)

With the whole of the day to fill children give the impression that much of what they are doing seems to them labour for its own sake rather than for understanding:

'If they give you a paragraph and if they asked you questions about

119

it, then if they let you write it in your own words, things would be better because at the moment you have to write in the same as it's got in the paragraph.'   (girl, primary)

Boredom can also set in because work is too demanding or left unexplained as well as because it appears routine:

'I don't like long discussions and things like that. Most of the time it's numbers. I like more explaining, more simple. I get stuck and muddled.'   (boy, primary)

Children do not automatically assume that school is the best or the most exciting place to work. They see the advantages of being free of the routine of the classroom:

'You learn more because you can see all things and you're allowed to take an insect book or a bird book or something, or an animal book . . . at the school we'll have to keep it there and work.'
                                                        (boy, primary)

'I like drawing and messing about with paint and doing experiments with paints and things. I always do things at home like that.'
                                                        (boy, secondary)

But then part of the problem of boredom in schools comes about because of the peculiarities of the timetable:

'It's so boring. We have these three lessons of it [science] on Wednesday. The practical is all right but the double lesson's really boring.'   (boy, secondary)

Using set books is associated in children's minds both with individual work and a lack of close involvement by the teacher. It replaces any sense of group cohesion and shared explanations.

Within school there are, it appears, different levels of work. There is the work that is so difficult that it cannot be understood. That is when boredom and resentment sets in, together with an antipathy to work. Then there are many pleasures within the classroom that do not seem to children to be part of the normal hard work of school; reading or art, or the pleasure of conversation. They tend to separate pleasure and work, as if work were always some kind of drudgery. When they do find something different and interesting they do not always associate it with work:

'After I've been on the computer I hate going back to start any work
again.'   (boy, secondary)

Boredom, therefore, is generally associated with work. But this
comes about gradually because of the experience of school.
Routine tasks and waiting for instructions are both dimensions of
learning that derive from the ways in which classrooms are
organized. The taste for 'interesting things to do' never leaves
children, but it is not always satisfied. Instead their experience
includes periods of frustration:

'The girls weren't able to get on with work 'cos he hadn't even given
out the sheets so you couldn't even carry on secretly.'
                                                     (girl, secondary)

The greatest frustration in the experience of work is a result not
just of routine work but of repetition. Children meet the same
topics again and again, and although they fear a new approach
and dread not understanding what is presented to them, they
equally resent the lack of organization that causes them to be told
the same things. This can happen because they are presented
with the same books:

'I get fed up with reading because I've read the book so many times,
the same one. It's a little thin story book, not a library book. I've read
it about three or four times so I won't forget it. So I learn the words
again.'   (girl, primary)

Sometimes it is the amount of time given to one subject that
causes the repetition:

'I'm not too keen on general studies because we're getting too much
of it because you get general studies at least twelve times a week . . .
we're doing prehistoric man . . . but the thing is I went through it all
in ____'s class.'   (girl, secondary)

Children commonly find themselves having to cover subjects
they have met before, either at a particular season of the year or
because there has been little overall management of the
curriculum. Whilst the National Curriculum may mitigate the
worst examples of repetition in the curriculum, like 'doing Anglo-
Saxons' three years running, the problem will remain:

'Every term we did nearly the same thing all the time and I've done

121

> co-ordinates at least five times now because I think I've done it since
> . . .'
>
> (boy, secondary)

> 'And the teacher keeps shouting — and when like in some subjects,
> we do the same *sort* of things each lesson, it gets boring.'
>
> (girl, secondary)

Repetition nearly always affects the kinds of task children are presented with. But it can also manifest itself in routine approaches to the subject, by undergoing the same topic, especially on transferring from one school to another:

> 'The three topics I've done in this school I've already done in my
> primary school. The only thing I've found different is in humanities
> which I haven't done before. But our next topic in humanities
> which is Eskimos and Red Indians, I've already done that, so I'm
> repeating another topic. I think it's silly. They should find out from
> your school what topics they've done and find some more ones that
> they haven't already done. They should have done something about
> that because there's ten of us who've already done that topic. You
> find they're ever so boring, because you've done it before.'
>
> (boy, secondary)

> 'I find I'm repeating most of the work I've done before. The topic
> work and the maths I've done before, at the same level.'
>
> (girl, secondary)

> 'When I was in the Infants we had the Ladybird books; by the second
> year I'd finished every single infant book they had so I had to go to
> the Lower Juniors. When I was in the Lower Juniors I finished all the
> books there so I had to get them from the Upper Juniors. In the
> Upper Juniors I nearly ran out of books. Because there was such a
> restricted thing and I found I was going ahead of everybody else.'
>
> (boy, secondary)

But this is not just the problem of a child too advanced for the poverty of resources. Work is repeated in style, as well as content.

The impression children give is that they are being held back by school and by the desire for standardization as if they all had to achieve the same levels of attainment. But then many teachers give children the impression that they spend a lot of time on one topic because of their insistence on repeating the facts, rather than finding out what the children already know:

'The teachers seem to go on about one subject instead of going straight from one to the next, so you spend more time on, say, Stone Age man . . . we'll be spending like two weeks on Neolithic whereas in my previous school we probably would have spent only two days on it.'   (girl, secondary)

'They just tell you things that you know and then keep telling you and they don't tell you anything different . . . if they tell you about the Earth or about Africa or something then they keep on telling you and they don't go on to something else like another country or anything.'
(boy, secondary)

When there is a lack of variety in the curriculum as well as in the presentation, children quickly lose interest.

The result for some children of not understanding what they are supposed to learn is far more traumatic than being bored. For several children school provides moments of great anguish:

'I've had quite a few tears about that because I get behind a lot.'
(girl, primary)

Children worry about falling behind, about not keeping up with their peer group. They are under pressure because their fear of failure is very strong:

'Sometimes I get worried about just a bit of English. It's my long division I get stuck on. I have to sit there and get worried and then I start shaking all over.'   (boy, primary)

It is difficult to suppose that such unhappiness and lack of confidence is conducive to academic progress. One of the reasons for the lack of development in the secondary school in the year after transfer might be the fact that for many of the children it is a traumatic experience, which they describe as 'scary' or 'petrifying'. But whilst there are many sources of fear, from teachers to bullies, traumas can also be found in unexpected places:

'I'm frightened of metalwork and woodwork. Because I don't like the things they use for metalwork. I saw a film where someone chopped their fingers off when he was doing woodwork . . . I don't like the machines they've got there and the kinds of stuff that sparkle and all that.'   (boy, secondary)

123

Apart from such specific fears most children are frightened of not being able to keep up with the demands of work. Boredom and fear are close allies:

'We get lots of work here but it's not really hard when you're not knowing about the things Mrs ____ does with us.'   (girl, primary)

From the point of view of children, the circumstances of the classroom are complex not only in terms of relationships but in terms of tasks which are sometimes clear and sometimes not. There is nothing static about the lessons, although children do long for stasis, the equilibrium of knowing what is expected of them. But for children the complexities of relationships in the classroom are not just those they have with the teacher but with each other. Children know that they can learn a great deal from each other. The routines of following a book or responding to the instructions of the teacher are often replaced as well as reinforced by the exchanges between children. These make the circumstances of classrooms include many different types of organization in which learning takes place:

'You do all different kinds of things, groups, pairs and on your own which she thinks the work is going to suit. One particular work suits a group, or you sit with a pair and another pair work and another pair. Then after the group she comes round each desk for a minute or two to discuss it with each one. In groups you learn what the other children know.'   (girl, primary

The main experience for children in the classroom is expressed not just in terms of the curriculum or of the teacher alone but in the way they work either with each other or individually. Their personal experience is blended with the experience of the group of friends. Children appreciate working together. Each of them stresses the importance of working with a friend or partner so that they can help each other over difficult tasks and take over the explanation from the teacher. For children the partner is a crucial factor in their learning, as important as the teacher or the subject. They never mention *other* people like ancillary staff or peripatetic teachers in the classroom, and do not mention the size of the class as a whole. But of all styles of classroom organization the possibility of working with someone else seems to them one of the most important, not because they just enjoy working with a friend, but because they feel they can receive help, give help and exchange ideas.[4]

'I work with my best friend . . . she helps me in the classroom and I help her.' (girl, primary)

'I work with Clare. I like that because you can talk to them. Say you get stuck, or say they get stuck, you can tell them to do it or you can work it out together.' (boy, primary)

The sense of personal achievement is not diminished by receiving help from another pupil. In nearly every case there is a sense of reciprocated help, of *sharing* rather than giving or receiving. Primary school children appreciate that they are allowed to work together. They are worried that when they go to the secondary school they will no longer be able to do so. To some extent this may be due to the fear of losing the chance to be with friends but it also derives from the sense that there will generally be less explanation and far more individual work.

'When you work with a partner it's good for you're doing things, studying, finding out things.' (girl, primary)

'If we are tidying something we work with a partner . . . 'cos it's nice 'cos you can talk to them and if you're stuck we can talk about it, or we ask them and help each other . . . I'd rather work with someone than alone.' (boy, primary)

'I like to work with one of my friends . . . I'd much rather prefer to have a partner to do it with. I like a partner to keep me company; they can help you if you get stuck.' (boy, primary)

'I like having a friend to work with because they can help you and you can help them. That makes me feel a bit more comfortable. I can get on without doing any mistakes but I can ask.' (girl, primary)

It is hard to ascertain how many teachers deliberately make use of the children's ability to explain to each other or whether this extra help is an accident that depends on the children's own initiative. Many teachers organize their classroom tasks in groups. The traditional management of learning has become centred on activities for groups of children whether organized around levels of ability or not. And yet teachers very rarely set up circumstances in which children can help each other. They do not arrange their groups so that they work collaboratively, with one child helping another.[5] It seems that children make use of the opportunity that group work gives to help each other. Although children are themselves a very important source of learning they are an under-used resource. Whilst teachers are often criticized for not matching tasks to children, and not extending all levels of ability, they are rarely encouraged to pay more attention to the potential of collaborative work.

It is clear from all the children's evidence that they create opportunities to talk to each other and that teachers allow them to do so. It is children who take the initiative in collaborative learning, they who seek help and give explanations. They are willing to receive help and realize that it is much easier to acquire individual attention from their partner than it is from the teacher, who has many children to deal with and who sometimes reverts to responding to those who queue at the desk. And there appears to be some security in knowing that other children can help, so that there is less disturbance to the teacher, let alone the rest of the class:

> 'If my friend is stuck we can help each other. I find that's better because your friend might find something out you don't know and she can help you and you might find something out that she didn't know and you can help each other.'
> (boy, primary)

Part of the hidden curriculum in working with a partner is the pleasure it gives. School is an opportunity for friendship, and the means of continuing such friendship even in work. Whilst the children make clear that they find the academic advantage of working with a partner is of the greatest significance, there are also less palpable advantages. Working with a partner is also good fun:

> 'On my topic work I work with David. I think I like working with a friend best. I'd like still to have a friend to work with when I go to the comp.'
> (boy, primary)

Sometimes the pleasure of working with a friend seems to outweigh the academic advantages:

'Like if we work in pairs always someone I pick. There's Robert. He's a comedian and he'll crack a joke and you'll have a laugh.'

(boy, primary)

In the secondary school finding someone to work with is a less permanent solution to sharing ideas:

'I used to sit by the window by the blackboard but now we've swapped places with another table sitting by the door or the shutters or whatever you call them . . . we don't usually ask the teacher: we just move around. . . . If you're sitting next to someone you could approach them . . . but they are short lessons anyway.'

(girl, secondary)

Although the reason for choosing places to sit and work is given as the friendship group — 'I just put myself there. All my friends were sitting there.' — the memory of the primary school experience of working with someone else over an extended period and learning from them, prevails:

'I tried my hardest in primary to get myself with my friends because they're all working a bit hard as well, and I had to even myself up a bit.'

(girl, secondary)

Learning from other people than the teacher, whether from groups or from individuals, is considered to be a normal part of school life. But it does not follow that it always happens, or that children expect it to happen automatically:

'I think we'll have to work on topic cards on our own. I think we'll have to work on our own at the comp. In one big class . . . you'll have to get on on your own. I'd rather have someone to work with.'

(boy, primary)

The idea of having someone to work with, to discuss ideas and share methods with, pervades many areas of children's school experience. They wish that the teacher could be someone who had time to discuss and explain, and give them individual attention, but they do not find this possible. Whether they work in large or small groups, children look for a chance to *share* ideas and feel that they learn as much from this as anything else. If there were one reform, within the circumstances of schools and classrooms, that would make a difference to children's experience

127

of learning it could well be this. Children seek the chance to talk, to argue about principles and about methods. They are naturally adept at explaining points to others. They therefore recognize the value of the working partner. What the teacher presents and explains is one thing, but what counts to pupils is the opportunity for discussion. Children dislike the isolation of work; they do not see themselves to be in secret competition:

'We work in groups and sometimes on our own, depending on what we're doing. We never worked with partners in Scotland. We worked individually all the time. It's better [here] than working individually all the time. It's more pleasant. If you're on your own and not working in a group you could get bored.'   (boy, primary)

The question remains whether children's desire to work together is seen as a pleasurable way of working, or whether it is a positive aid to their levels of achievement. Their motivation is certainly increased. Children like to work with a friend. But such a means of working does not arise purely out of self-indulgence, of wishing to have an 'easy' time. They appreciate the usefulness of working in a group for the sake of work. A group in their eyes can be defined as anything between three and ten, but it is usually fairly small. They are aware of the distinction between working closely with one other person, so that they can have a conversation, and a large group where a different level of discussion takes place and where one person can dominate the rest, like a chairman or teacher:

'I don't mind working with about two people, but if it becomes more than that I get annoyed because it's too much ... I sit with my friend.'   (girl, secondary)

'I like to do it in small groups really because if you're in a big group and you had a day off you'd be behind everybody else but if there's just a little small group of about four you all stick together.'
                                           (girl, primary)

In a small group the prevailing atmosphere is that of helping each other and of having a defined role. This is why the 'group' size is defined not so much in terms of numbers as in terms of the style of working, of helping each other:

'When we are making something we work in groups and our topic is working in pairs, or threes.' (boy, primary)

'We work in groups when we're going on to something new and no one knows how to do it . . . when you work with a partner it's good.'
(girl, primary)

The group is a matter of mutual help, or working on 'topics' or experiments:

'We work on our own for some maths. But if we are experimenting we work with groups and we work with a partner.' (boy, primary)

'We work it out for ourselves in a little group.' (girl, primary)

The alternative to being instructed by the teacher is the help given to each other. The pleasure children have in 'experiments' in different ways of working is partly because of their interest in collaboration. Children assume that it is difficult to work out things by themselves; to 'work' it out with others is always the major alternative to having things explained by the teacher. Groups are seen as the alternative to distant lecturing styles:

'The teacher will use a blackboard if we all get stuck on the same thing. She'll keep us as one class . . . it's better in groups.'
(girl, primary)

Children appreciate the educational advantages of working with partners. They also know that for several reasons, including the avoidance of distractions and the singleness of competition, there are dangers inherent in working with a partner. And there are times when the teacher uses groups not so much to enable children to help each other but as a means of organization for its own sake:

'Brown group is still doing about fractions. Now we're doing about area, perimeter. I don't really like doing school much.'
(boy, primary)

'We work table by table.' (girl, primary)

There are occasions when working with a friend is seen as a definite disadvantage that interferes with work:

'I sat down there and a friend sat next to me but she kept talking to me so she was moved away.' (girl, secondary)

> 'The girl I am friends with . . . she mucks about in class, you know. Sometimes she's all right, but . . .' (girl, primary)

Children are aware that such a way of working can be a distraction from learning 'by themselves'. There are times when they do not want to share, and want to make progress on their own initiative. In a group they know it is too easy to rely on the person who knows most:

> 'If you're in a group you can help each other and stuff like that. I think it'll be better to work things out for yourself actually.'
> (girl, primary)

> 'I work on my own sometimes. I do art in groups but . . . they copy you.' (boy, primary)

Children become increasingly apprehensive of helping others as they enter the secondary school. They assume that the much-cherished sharing which characterizes the primary classroom will be replaced. At first they might move 'next to a friend' for security. But they know that the working practices of secondary schools are more individualistic, more competitive. And they then discover that secondary schools make no point of exploiting the resource of children themselves. This is partly because the growing stress on exams and qualifications enhances the need for individual achievement. Some children therefore work by themselves because '. . . with maths there's nobody as high as me.' The competitiveness that arises from awareness of markedly different levels of achievement (they always know about different levels of ability) makes collaborative working less likely. Children are aware of many motives when teachers organize the class.

This includes the disciplinary matter of having to work by themselves, as punishment:

> 'I work in groups, sometimes you work alone. I do if I'm doing drawing or if you have to do English work. The teacher don't like you in the class 'cos you're disturbing all the other children . . . so you're sent into another classroom or sit in the corner. Then you work on your own. I'm on a table on me own because I'm always messing around so I have to go on another table.' (boy, primary)

Very rarely do children suggest, however, that they can always 'work better on my own'. Despite their concern with disruption and competition, children see the value of mutual co-operation. They think that they have more and better ideas if they can test them on others.

Nevertheless, despite the acknowledged dangers of group work and the recognition of the benefits of collaboration, children are very aware of school as an area of competition. There is a certain pressure on children *not* co-operating because of their recognition that they are going to be individually assessed. Children are aware of how much they can get away with and how important is the reaction of teachers to their work. They see the tension between the desire not to work and the constant scrutiny they are under. This becomes the more intense as they get older. Children accept the need to fulfil obligations, to provide what is demanded (when they know what that is). They accept that work 'has to be done' for all kinds of reasons. In fact one of the phrases that children cite as typical of teachers is 'do it again':

> 'It was important as long as you did it right. Then you handed it up, and you go to another subject, you finish that, then you have to go back on to the other subject which hasn't been marked, so that at the end of the week when the teacher goes home she'd got about five sets of subject in the book when she could have done it every day. It was important because you've got to do it, you've got to make sure it's done . . . so you know you're not going to get behind, you know you won't be the class fool and things like that.'   (girl, secondary)

Children feel that they must not only keep up, but have work which is appropriately demanding; they do not like it if 'some of the work here is too easy'. There are even times when a teacher prevents a child doing work on their own level:

> 'I got this card out and I was doing it. It was really interesting and quite hard — but after I found I'd taken out the wrong card — the teacher said it was too difficult, too high a level.'   (girl, secondary)

Children have a clear idea of their own abilities, and readily acknowledge those who are better than them, as well as those who are worse:

> 'I'd put myself somewhere between the middle and the top, I'm good

131

> but I'm not absolutely perfect. I think there are people in the class who are better than me.'
> (girl, secondary)

They also find that the chance to work in pairs gives them a spur to compete:

> 'I work hard because Joanne's a bit faster than me and I don't like that, in humanities at any rate.'
> (girl, secondary)

In the first year of secondary school the aspect of competition that strikes children most forcibly is the question of 'merit' and 'effort' marks, of which all of them seem to approve, whether they are themselves one of the 'best' or not:

> 'I'd say in the middle, with a few people who can do it more easily than I can — just a few of them. There's a girl, Andrea, and she's good. She got a commendation in the first few weeks of being there . . . I've got two merit marks and half an effort mark . . . I'm looking forward to getting it.'
> (girl, secondary)

'Effort' marks are a good sign and accepted as a just reward. Children scrutinize the work that is handed back to them for the mark, *or* the comment:

> ''Cos you don't know if you've got it all wrong. "See me" it says or "Finish" or else you could have an effort mark — one effort mark — gold star, even, that's all right sometimes. . . .'
> (boy, secondary)

For a number of children the gaining of an effort mark is a highlight of their experience at school, especially when they appear before the assembly to have it acknowledged.

Children's views of school are, within the complexity of individual differences, consistent, as has been noted before, despite differences in gender. This consistency includes their analysis of one matter on which they all notice clear discrimination. All children recognize that boys are treated differently by teachers:

> 'They tell a boy off more than a girl when they've done the same thing.'
> (girl, secondary)

> 'They shout at the boys but they just speak to the girls . . . I mean it's all right if you are a girl, but I suppose if you're a boy it's not.'
> (girl, primary)

'They tell the girls off more mildly. It's not fair. They get away with things.'   (boy, secondary)

'In class when the girls do things wrong they don't get told off. The teachers take no notice.'   (boy, primary)

Such a consistent recognition of discrimination is underlined by the acceptance that boys *deserve* to be treated differently, that it is in their nature to be more volatile, more talkative and more disobedient:

'The boys are quite naughty — the girls sit quietly and get on with their work. Some chat, but they do work.'   (girl, primary)

'They don't really tell the girls off so much. I suppose the girls don't misbehave so much.'   (boy, primary)

If the children themselves make assumptions about behaviour patterns, they assume that teachers will do the same, that the treatment meted out to the different sexes is a result of different expectations of behaviour:

'They expect the girls to be a bit better at doing the work, and they sometimes tell the boys off more than the girls. The girls sometimes get away with things. They expect the boys to be naughty and the girls to be good.'   (girl, secondary)

Many of the children feel that the teachers are easily deceived, that they suffer from a self-fulfilling prophecy, driving the boys to be worse than they are, and ignoring what the girls do:

'If it's a girl who asks to go to the toilet, he lets them. If it's a boy he shouts at them, and he shouts at them, the boys, for being noisy, but not the girls.'   (boy, primary)

'They expect the boys to be naughty and not behave, but they don't see the girls misbehaving — well, they don't seem to notice. They yell at the boys more.'   (boy, secondary)

It is not only boys who notice such discrimination:

'They think that the boys are so naughty they sit at the front and the girls are so good they sit at the back, but sometimes it's not true 'cos some of the girls are very naughty — like me — the boys are told off more than the girls, even if the girls are doing the same sort of thing.'
                                                                   (girl, primary)

Boys and girls in the early experiences of secondary school resent
the consistent differences between the way they are treated at a
variety of levels. Boys obviously find this kind of discrimination
annoying, as if they were forced to be typecast as a group who
had no wish to learn, but was intent on disruption:[6]

> 'Mostly the girls get better treatment. I'm not offending the boys, but
> mostly the girls — bit of a shame — 'course they get out first; they
> don't get told off as much as the boys.'   (boy, secondary)

> 'I think they treat the girls much better than the boys for some reason.
> Why do the girls get more privileges than us? In humanities the girls
> can sit together on the same table. The boys can't do that. That's not
> fair. Boys are a bit noisy sometimes, but really they're just the same.'
>   (boy, secondary)

It is not only the boys who resent the discrimination. There are
occasions when the girls find the privileges given to them
something of a disadvantage, as it fosters the stereotypes of male
strength:

> ''Cos the boys they get treated as if they're really bad. They're always
> being shouted at, sometimes for doing things that they haven't even
> done, and they're not liked, like the girls. The girls — some of the men
> teachers, they let the boys do all the work, like taking the chairs back,
> when all the class should have been doing it, and they let the girls
> watch.'   (girl, secondary)

> 'Like in drama — the teacher thinks girls are weak, so they can't put
> chairs away and things like that. He says — "No you sit down, the
> boys can do it." And they have to put the chairs away and things. We
> shout at the teacher and say "Why can't we?" 'cos after, the boys pick
> on us. They say "Look — see — admit that you're weak."'
>   (girl, secondary)

Such discriminations are also a part of the learning experience of
children. They learn the assumptions that quiet, well-behaved
girls work hard, and that boys are naughty and destructive. It is
interesting to note how the boys take up the cue from the drama
teacher. The children clearly find such stereotyping bewildering
at times, but although it comes out most clearly in the secondary
school, it is apparent earlier:

'The teacher likes the girls. The girls don't get started fighting and swearing. Some of the boys get your nerves on edge and you get really mad and you start saying things to them or sticking your pencil into them. Miss normally lets the girls do things like giving out the books or give out the papers. . . . She looks angry at me. Sometimes I'm in trouble. Some of the boys just make me get really angry and when I try to go up and tell Miss they won't even listen or the other boys try and stop me.'
(boy, primary)

Much of what children learn in school has only an oblique connection with the formal curriculum. Even within the classroom they observe implicit assumptions about social roles.[7] They notice that girls and high achievers have a particularly comfortable relationship with teachers.[8] They detect the differences of response to boys and girls, and know that low-achieving boys are the group that receives the most strenuous negative attention.

Very few of the principles that underlie social behaviour — issues of gender or control — are ever discussed in the curriculum. For this reason children rely on each other to discuss and analyse their perceptions of society. The formal curriculum, with its strong emphasis on language and mathematics and on the acquisition of knowledge, rarely enters the world of speculation, rarely addresses those very issues that most worry children. This vacuum is filled by children talking to each other.

Children learn from each other both about social attitudes and about the formal curriculum. They are, in fact, a potent source of learning, when given the chance. Children who are 'high attainers' do particularly well in group work, and relish the chance to discuss issues.[9] They help others, unless they are given the chance to choose between the stimulation of an equally bright friend or a slower one, in which case the latter would be ignored. Children work co-operatively quite naturally.[10] Even without special preparation the idea of helping each other is taken for granted, and seen to be helpful. It is only after a number of years that such co-operation is drilled out of them. When used as 'teachers' children discover not only a natural propensity to help, but gain by doing so.[11] For them explanation is a way of exploring ideas. They learn by trying to communicate.

Working in groups, or in pairs, is one of the most enjoyable

135

and beneficial experiences of learning. When children are allowed to pursue topics and develop ideas they can show a genuine excitement at the experience. When the opportunities are created by the teacher, children demonstrate the capacity to teach and learn, to analyse and communicate. But not all classroom discussion is like that. Often the talk that takes place is desultory. It fills gaps, rather than being itself part of the lesson. And then talk is a relief from the tedium of work rather than part of work.

Although children find collaboration constructive and rewarding, their experience of learning nevertheless remains lonely, and private. This is partly because of the conditions of classrooms and assemblies; the larger the number in a group of people, the more isolated the individual. But it is also partly a result of children's growing awareness of competition, of distinctions between levels of ability and success with teachers. And it is partly because children are not encouraged over the years to talk about what they learn. When they do talk about their own learning, their awareness of what they learn, as well as how, increases significantly.[12] But gradually success is measured in different ways, and the sense of potential failure grows stronger. As children get older so their rating of their own intellectual abilities declines.[13] Their ideas of what makes for success also change significantly. Young children rate their ability to learn as being a matter of effort, mastery of their subject and social reinforcement. Older children view success in terms of measured achievement. They learn to label each other and moderate themselves. It is then that the experience of learning is closely associated not with pleasure but with failure.

NOTES AND REFERENCES

1. See Bennett, N., Desforges, C., Cockburn, A. and Wilkinson, B. *The Quality of Pupil Learning Experiences*. London: Lawrence Erlbaum, 1984, for a devastating analysis.
2. A survey of five schools in the Midlands, which followed children through a whole school day, concluded that no less than 82 per cent of the time was spent waiting for something to happen (see earlier chapters).
3. Thomas, N. 'Class teaching and curriculum support.' In C. Cullingford, *The Primary Teacher*. London: Cassell, 1989, pp. 37–55.

4. Studies show how successful even self-directed groups can be. Ghaye, A. 'Outer appearances with inner experiences: towards a more holistic view of group work.' *Educational Review* **38** (1), 45–56, 1986.

5. Bronfenbrenner, U. *Two Worlds of Childhood*. London: Routledge, 1971.

6. Pollard's 'gangs' in *The Social World of the Primary School* (London: Holt, Rinehart and Winston, 1985) consist largely of boys. Girls find other ways of avoiding conformity.

7. Sharp, R. and Green, A. *Education and Social Control*. London: Routledge and Kegan Paul, 1975.

8. Worrall, N. and Tsarna, H., 'Teachers' reported practices towards girls and boys in science and languages.' *British Journal of Educational Psychology* **57** (3), 300–312, 1987.

9. Bennett, N. and Cass, A. 'The effects of group composition on group interactive processes and pupil understanding.' *British Educational Research Journal* **15** (1), 19–32, 1988.

10. Burden. M., Emsley, M. and Constable, H. 'Encouraging progress in collaborative group work.' *Education 3–13* **16** (1), 51–56, 1988.

11. Atherley, C.A. ' "Shared Reading": an experiment in peer tutoring in the primary classroom.' *Educational Studies* **15** (2), 145–153, 1989.

12. Pramling, I. 'Developing children's thinking about their own learning.' *British Journal of Educational Psychology* **58** (3), 266–278, 1988.

13. Stipek, D. and MacIver, D. 'Developmental change in children's assessment of intellectual competence.' *Child Development* **60** (3), 521–538, 1989.

CHAPTER 9
The Formal School Curriculum

'I usually finish first and she says "Now what can you do?" and she stands and thinks and I think "How long is this going on?", and she goes "Right, you can help me," and I had to paint strips of paper. It was very boring.'   (girl, secondary)

In the many relationships and the varieties of experience in the classroom, some central facts are manifest. The class is organized by the teacher and the subjects that are being studied are controlled by the teacher. Children might learn in their own way but the curriculum presented to them is not a matter of choice. Whether imposed on the teacher from outside or not, the curriculum is, as far as the children are concerned, what the teacher chooses it to be. They accept what is given to them as a body of knowledge, facts to be learned and skills to be acquired. They recognize the different levels of attention paid to different subjects by the amount of time spent on them and the time of day in which they are presented but they all accept the fact that the formal curriculum is what they are in school to acquire.[1]

This acceptance of a body of knowledge does not necessarily help teachers. The subjects would be less 'closed' if there were more questions about the purpose. For whilst there are many kinds of subject within a lesson, there are few choices that children make. They must do their maths and their writing. They see this as part of the routine of school. They do not notice the uneven distribution of time given to geography or history compared to the 'core' of skills.[2] Although they wish for variety in learning methods and clarity of teaching style, the general approach to work is to accept what is given.

The psychology of acceptance which pervades classrooms leads not to assiduous attention but to strategies of secret avoidance. It is another explanation of the amount of time that is spent waiting, for all depends on the next instruction the teachers will give. And the more teachers deliver a curriculum based on national agreement the more they will accept the assumption that all analysis of what a curriculum should consist of, and why, has already been covered. Whilst children form their own views, and gradually question what the curriculum is for, they essentially accept it as given during their central years at school.

Children feel themselves to be in a system in which one thing leads to another. They are prepared by primary schools for secondary, by secondary schools for jobs or higher education. They do not go from one to another before the allotted time. What they learn, therefore, appears to them to consist of a gradual accretion of knowledge; a curriculum that seems related to age. To go beyond its expectations is not, for children, particularly viable or, indeed, respectable. Success for them is norm related. And the formal curriculum presents its own inexorable momentum.

The curriculum does not, however, appear to children to be a highly organized affair. On the contrary it can appear fairly arbitrary. It is controlled and organized very differently according to the wishes of various teachers. Despite the dominance of maths and English it seems to divide itself not according to what the subjects are for, but the way they are taught. The central use of topics as a means of organizing does not lead children to detect the holistic nature of the curriculum. Instead they see what they are given as a series of small tasks. Some subjects are known to be demanding in terms of the amount of writing that needs to be done, or in the secrets of their techniques, but these vary from pupil to pupil. Some subjects are attractive when they provide practical activities rather than the same routines. The sense of movement from one thing to another, which is symbolized by the organization of subject specialist classrooms in secondary school, is also implicit in the primary school as the day is broken up between different demands for different groups.

In the absence of any analysis of the purpose underlying different parts of the curriculum children draw their own conclusions about which might be relevant. They accept what is given and then try to ascertain a purpose. Thus mathematics has a part to play in developing a long-term future:

'I'm going to be a vet. if I can be a vet. and maths will help me with medicine and things . . . maths helps you when you're shopping.'
(boy, primary)

It also has a more immediate part to play in everyday experience.

139

But children rarely connect subjects with their lives outside the classroom. They like to make connections when they can:

'I like maths because you can work out how much money you've spent in the shops.'   (girl, primary)

but these are rare afterthoughts. Generally the subjects they do in school are done for their own sake, and the pleasures they have are in the activities:

'Science is fun especially when you're doing things.' (girl, primary)

If the applicability of a subject in everyday life is rarely considered the sense of what all parts of the curriculum are *for* is not:

'To get a job you have to know English, science, history, maths and spelling.'   (boy, primary)

There appears to be a gap between the day-to-day experience of the curriculum and the sense of purpose that explains its existence. In the experience of children, teachers rarely mention why they are learning a particular subject. They tend to be 'doing English for the teacher'. This assumption that the curriculum is a given entity and accepted as such is pointed up by the way in which new subjects, such as economic understanding, are introduced in *addition* to the National Curriculum. When the National Curriculum was first being discussed in terms of principles, attention was constantly given to its breadth and balance.[3] All the arguments centred on the amount of time to be given to a traditional list of subjects in order to achieve that 'balance'. Whilst there was an acceptance that the way of teaching would be left to the individual teacher, there was just as strong an assumption that the curriculum is a given entity, to be delivered and assessed in prescribed quantities.

Children explore their own means of learning, whether they are aware of their own style or not, whether they are holistic or serial learners, for example.[4] They are driven by complex motivations, by interest in teachers or pressure from their peers. In crucial areas of learning it is very difficult to know exactly how the individual learns. A skill like reading is symbolic of much of learning. It is much researched. But whether the emphasis seems to be on the association of clues, the analysis of text, the understanding of phonemes or of codes, it is clear that children find their *own* means of learning.[5] They are greatly aided by intelligent teaching and sensitive diagnosis. They are not always helped by being confronted by a particular belief or technique.

This gap between teaching and learning is apparent in the formal curriculum of school. The timetable symbolizes not only the value of different subjects but the acceptance of a given set of subjects. For children the work they do does not need to have a reason. It is a *donné* that they are 'doing' what the teacher tells them to do. Despite the best endeavours to create interesting thematic material through topics or 'schemes of work', children see the subjects traditionally, as separate, distinct and unintegrated. Just as their work has few connections with the world outside, so it has few connections with other subjects. They know when they are doing maths, science of geography. They are aware of all the different elements that make up English. And such recognition of different subjects is as strong in the primary as the secondary school.

The work that is done in schools often seems disconnected. Different groups may be undergoing different subjects at the same time, or classes may be moving rapidly from the science block to music. But this is what children take for granted. Because they do not analyse the curriculum and its purpose, relevance remains for them some very obscure connection between a subject and the world of work:

'I'd rather be at work. Some of the things you learn in school might help you working on a farm . . . but history and geography doesn't.'
(girl, primary)

The difference between school work and their subsequent experience can strike them forcibly because it is rarely explored.[6] Moral, spiritual and aesthetic values are *assumed* to be covered by the curriculum as it stands. Children take a pragmatic stance.

The curriculum is what teachers offer. In the primary classrooms all the demarcations of time and task are signalled by the teacher:

'It was like when the teacher said, "Now we're going to do maths," and stuff like that.'
(boy, secondary)

The signals are essentially about time; warnings that a change will come, time to finish work, time to prepare the next stage. In the secondary school the signals are at one remove:

> 'You come in at a quarter to nine and the tannoy tells you something and you get on with your work.' (boy, secondary)

By that means the notion of different, separate subjects is reinforced, long before the need to specialize. And long before the advent of the subject specialist children have analysed the different characteristics of the curriculum, not just in the separate bodies of knowledge, but in different demands of skill and response. It needs no consultant to teach them that.[7]

Although the curriculum in schools is characterized by demarcations, it is also dominated by a central core of maths and English. In the light of the repeated calls for a greater concentration on a central core this is ironic.[8] Primary schools spend the bulk of their time concentrating on the 'three Rs'. All major surveys have revealed the dominance, in terms of energy, expertise and time, of reading and, especially, writing and mathematics.[9] Indeed the Primary Survey of 1978 expressed concern that the curriculum being offered was so narrow that little attention was being paid to subjects such as geography and history.[10] More recently the victim of such dominance has been felt to be science. But for children the importance of the central core, a view shared by their parents, is acknowledged and part of their experience:

> 'I suppose English and maths are the most important ones.'
> (girl, secondary)

This is acknowledged in status and time. Children accept that the status given to them is because of their practical relevance:

> 'Maths and English are the most important because they help you learn a lot and if you, say, went to work in a newsagent's you have to have maths and for other jobs you need English.' (boy, secondary)

The dominance of the core subjects in primary schools is such that children look forward to the variety of offerings that secondary schools appear to make. The narrow curriculum confined to one room is contrasted to the possibility of specialized laboratories and lavish equipment:

'Different subjects other than maths and English. We could do
something like history.'   (boy, primary)

'Here we don't have much history and geography but at the comp.
you'll have it about four times a week.'   (boy, primary)

The absence of particular subjects from the consciousness of
children is exacerbated by the fact that when a teacher thinks
they are included, as in topic work, they are not necessarily
recognized:

'Well, we do history but we don't have lessons in history. We have
like environmental studies, like a topic.'   (boy, primary)

The clearer definitions of subjects in the secondary school is part
of the ethos of 'real learning' that children feel takes place there,
and for which primary schools are preparing them. Children are
concerned that the curriculum in primary schools can be narrow
and monotonous. It does not seem demanding and is also
generally unvaried.

From the point of view of the individual pupil there are many
experiences that seem to be monotonous. But they are also part
of the rhythm of a school. The day is broken into simple periods
of time; a time for work and a time for play. The school year is
also defined by notions of time, with seasonal topics from Easter
to Christmas, and the periods between terms. Although the use of
time is a subjective matter — 'wasted time' — the fact that it is
controlled and manipulated by teachers and the timetable makes
it an almost impersonal regulation. The time to 'work', defined as
writing or maths, fills up part of the day with a regular pattern.
In that time all that is done is defined as work. Contrasting topics
all fulfil this regular monotony.

Time has a subjective element but it is also one of the symbols
of power. Just as 'time is money', so control over time is power.
To this extent children recognize what teachers feel to be most
important and what weight they give to different subjects.
Nowhere is this more apparent than in mathematics, which
appears from its placing in the day to lie at the heart of the school
curriculum.[11] Children recognize the 'work' of school as
consisting of writing and arithmetic.

Whether children like mathematics or not, they find the

subject 'necessary' and 'relevant'. They also find it demanding. They share with their parents the sense of its importance and utility. And they see, in mathematics, some sense of continuity between primary and secondary school. It is, to them, a coherent subject, with defined boundaries. It is also a subject they tend to either love or hate. With mathematics children know clearly where they stand. They know that as they progress they will be given ever harder versions of what they are doing already, which either pleases or worries them:

> 'I was looking at my brother's maths book and it looked really hard. There were sums like 13,000 to the power of 10 and all that. Horrible. I hated looking in it.' (boy, primary)

But the subject still remains a distinct one even if it is approached in a different way:

> 'Up there they'll teach you different ways of doing maths so that's more important.' (boy, primary)

In secondary schools they expect to find 'different things altogether' as well as 'maths, harder maths and English'.

Those who find maths difficult take for granted that this difficulty will not be overcome, as if it is a subject they are either naturally good at or not:

> 'I don't like maths lessons because I'm not very good and I find it harder than any other subject because I keep getting mixed up.' (girl, primary)

Mathematics is a subject that makes clear demands of a particular kind. Even when all other subjects seem an easy pleasure, mathematics stands out:

> 'It's mostly easy at the primary, except maths.' (boy, primary)

The children explain that their approach to mathematics depends on their aptitude:

> 'I like it and I think because I like it. Most people are good if they like it and if they can't do it, they hate it. A bit like writing.' (boy, primary)

The connection between liking a subject and being good at it is always close. Those who like mathematics know that they are in command of what they are doing. It does not seem to make varied demands. Those who like the subject like the fact that it has easily assessed outcomes. They know that once they can 'do their sums' they are secure in the achievement. Once understanding is reached, so is mastery:

'I like maths because I can understand it.'　　　　(girl, primary)

Mathematics is understood by children to be a series of similar problems and techniques that they enjoy doing if they understand them:

'I like maths and I can get them right and it's a lot easier to cope with than English and that.'　　　　(boy, primary)

Mathematics is not only a defined subject but a secure one in that once the techniques are mastered examples can be repeated. It therefore seems easy to some:

'That's the thing I'm best at. Maths is the easiest for me.'
　　　　(girl, primary)

'It's my favourite because I can do it very well.'　　　(boy, primary)

All enthusiasts for mathematics reiterate their *own* ability to cope. They do not think so much of the subject itself as their own prowess. Mathematics gives them something to do:

'I like number work and you get to do sort of making things as well as maths where you don't much in English. You do things in maths.'
　　　　(boy, primary)

Children stress the attractiveness of a subject that stresses the importance of correctness, of having clear answers, right or wrong, and problems to be solved:

'I like number work. I like solving problems. Problem maths. You've got to use your brain and think and when it comes to problems I like working them out. I think the way you do things helps you to like it.'
　　　　(boy, primary)

Mathematics comes easily to some children. But for those who do not understand the necessary techniques it is a subject which seems to shut them out completely. This also underlines the

145

associations children have between mathematics and repeated sums; doing something again and again. Those who cannot do so face repeated failure:

'I'm worried about the maths. Like fractions or anything you don't understand.'   (girl, primary)

Just as those who can do sums feel secure in the repeated awards, so those who cannot find it a worrying, even traumatic, experience:

'I'm just getting a bit worried at the maths. It's the only subject I worry about. It's my long division I get stuck on. I have to sit there and get worried and then I start shaking all over.'   (boy, primary)

Children feel that if they do not understand the subject easily there will be no hope of them ever doing it well. They anticipate failure because of lack of ability:

'I don't like maths because I'm not good at them. I just don't like learning maths. If I'm interested in something I like it. It's the way you do it.'   (girl, primary)

'I don't really like maths because some of the questions; they ask you really hard questions and you don't get them.'   (boy, primary)

Children's attitude to mathematics encompasses an acceptance of its importance and a sense that they either like it and are good at it or not. For they associate mathematics with a series of arithmetical problems that become harder the older they get. They rarely think of geometry or theoretical aspects of maths. They assume that the demands of the secondary school will differ mostly in degree. For those who find maths difficult the prospect is frightening. For those to whom it comes easily the prospect is of pursuing different approaches. Again, this underlines the association of maths with routine. At primary school they expect to do a great deal of arithmetic. They then hope that the secondary school will make new demands:

'The lessons won't be the same but there'll be maths. Maths here is long division. Multiplication. You'll have a lot more harder fractions at the comp. I'm sure they'll teach you the same.'   (girl, primary)

For some children — the mathematically gifted — secondary

school presents the opportunity of engaging in new problems. They look forward to different styles of presentation and different kinds of question. But they find much that is familiar; similar sums but more complicated:

> 'Well some are harder. In maths we're doing co-ordinates. Well we've done that but they're teaching us is a more complicated way, and when we get up to the fifth year they'll know what we're on about and that.'   (boy, secondary)

The problem is that children find themselves repeating the kinds of work they have done before. This can be a pleasure for it makes mathematics an easy subject, but it does not suggest that the levels of demand are very high. The place of mathematics in the timetable is secure, but the material is familiar:

> 'Now every couple of weeks we're doing different things but there every term we did nearly the same thing at the same time and I've done co-ordinates at least five times now.'   (girl, secondary)

The appeal of mathematics lies in the clarity of the tasks, and the ease with which some children can be successful. But even to them, mathematics can be a routine. All children find much of the material repetitive. For those who fail, such failure is drilled in. But those who succeed also find the worksheets or books presented to them too easy to be stimulating:

> 'We just work off cards and it's too easy, just copying cards out.'
> (boy, secondary)

> 'Maths I don't like . . . it's boring. All that getting up and going to get cards. I just don't like it.'   (girl, secondary)

To children in schools, mathematics is one of the subjects most typical of their experience. It is considered essential, but is part of the routine. It is something to be 'done' either with pleasure or with difficulty. It is dependent on the resources given out by the teacher — work cards, books or sheets. The consistent underlying response of children is to see maths as a series of tasks to be carried out. It has few direct connections with the world outside but is *assumed* to have significance, to be 'useful' for tasks like shopping. This level of acceptance is true of those who like

147

maths and those who do not. When the tasks presented are interesting then the subject becomes interesting too:

'We do SMILE and we have a choice of cards and they're not just boring maths; they're fun and we have a different card each time.'
(girl, secondary)

For most pupils, however, the tasks raise no such excitement. They remain 'just boring maths'.

'We just do lots and lots of sheets — some of them seem the same.'
(boy, secondary)

Mathematics is a subject with fixed methods and very clear outcomes. Children know where they are with it, whether they like it or not. English is a very different matter. Children see it as a less defined entity with a greater complexity of demands. Whereas they know whether they are good at maths, or not, they are far less certain with English. They know that it is also one of the 'core' subjects that dominate the timetable. But they are also aware that it consists of different levels of demand and different kinds of task. What pleases the teacher in maths is clear. But success in English is far more difficult to define. There is no automatic reward for being right. And the subject is divided between the testable tasks — writing, essentially — and all the other uses of language which are also involved, from talking to reading.

Children know that maths is about numbers as English is about words. But the tests that define a subject are more varied. There are comprehension tests and dictations. They need to express individual ideas as well as present accurate spellings. They know whether they are good at maths, but in English there is always something opaque:

'Writing; I can't really get the right words. I can't really get big words in. Maths is the easiest for me.' (girl, primary)

Up to a point English also has simple, assessable components. But children never quite know their own abilities to do well in them. It is the task itself that dominates:

'I don't like English that much. I like writing stories but doing English off the board sometimes get a bit boring, when you're doing

148

the same things over and over again. But I know it's important. I don't think you can do English a different way. You just have to put up with it.'   (boy, secondary)

Children accept the need to do the given tasks, however repetitive. 'You just have to put up with it.' They also assume that what they do is important, even if the purpose is to serve another subject:

'You do spelling and spelling helps you with maths because sometimes you have to write things down in maths.' (girl, primary)

It is the separate components of English that strike children as having significance. These 'components', however, consist not only of subjects such as 'spelling' but a round of exercises of different kinds. It is a subject that lacks any sense of overall purpose and that relies on familiar routines. One of the routines is spelling:

'Lately I got quite low, right, because the fourth-year words I get are quite hard. The third-years have their words. Spelling is difficult. I've had a cry but on my own. I don't let anybody see.' (boy, primary)

Another is reading a story, collectively:

'You know, when you read a story and it just goes on and on and you're going round in circles, round the class.'   (boy, secondary)

But the routines that are most associated with English are those exercises which derive from textbooks:

'I don't like English. Well, you have to answer all these questions and I don't like doing that. It's an English book. That's the only thing I don't like, and topic. You get these books, right, and there's a sheet with all the questions on....'   (girl, primary)

Standard practice for those who are 'doing English' is as dependent on printed sheets as maths:

'I get fed up with English sometimes because we do English exercises and they are mostly all the same because they give you a paragraph of writing and you have to answer questions on it and we do that twice a week and it's just because it's a bit boring.' (girl, primary)

Those children who do not like English find the subject dull and the underlying purpose of the tasks obscure. It is as if there were

149

a code to the subject which is as arcane as maths. The tasks that need to be carried out are done because school demands it. So the comfortable routine of school can become dull:

> 'We do the same sort of thing in each lesson. It gets boring.'
>
> (girl, secondary)

Those children who do enjoy English discover a sense of personal ownership.[12] Instead of having to complete set tasks they can pursue ideas of their own:

> 'Because you are allowed to write a story that you want to write. Say you've finished, you're allowed to draw a picture about it.'
>
> (boy, primary)

Once children acquire a sense of possession over their own work, it is no longer perceived as routine. The excitement of new discovery that was lacking in their comments on maths *can* be seen occasionally in their responses to English:

> 'I like creative writing. It sharpens your skills. It makes you want to be a poet. It's ideas. I like getting my ideas. Sometimes you get given something to write about and you get your own ideas about it. Sometimes you're finding things out in your mind and searching your mind.'
>
> (girl, primary)

The limitation of English as presented to children is its reliance on exercises. Sometimes such routines are easier to accept than anything more demanding:

> 'I don't really like English much ... I like SS — spelling and sentences.' (boy, primary)

But the distinctions between creative writing and 'Junior English books and comprehension' are clear. Children can feel threatened by one just as they can be bored by the other. Relatively few children positively enjoy English. When they do it is because of the pleasures they can derive not from school exercises but from the private satisfactions of the world of literature, their own and other people's:

> 'In English I like reading and he lets you if you finish. We, like, read to the sixth-formers on Thursdays, and if your own school book gets boring we can bring our own books. I think that's a good idea.'
>
> (girl, secondary)

'Reading, because you get to read a lot of books and it calms you down a bit.'   (girl, primary)

For enthusiasts, English is a chance to discover the world of the imagination. It is a subject that allows personal statements. It is also a subject that many children worry about because its tasks are not clearly defined. What exactly is it that will satisfy the teacher? Once this is discovered, the children feel themselves unleashed:

'You have to think with the senses and emotions, like the octopus she put on the board. Sometimes you're thinking about something like a spider and you can actually feel you're there and you can actually see that horrible spiky thing. You can feel it. You can use your imagination.'   (boy, secondary)

For each child who discovers the pleasures of using the imagination there are many who still associate English with tasks such as spelling and comprehension. They are inhibited by all the skills they must learn without any clear sense of their purpose. Children do not anticipate that their experiences will be very different in the secondary school. English might be 'more difficult' but it is envisaged as being so 'because it'll be a different book'. In the end the subject is as bound up by the application of certain skills, like spelling, as maths is. The realization of the purpose of using such skills is limited to a few of the children. Just as mathematics can become a routine of repetitive work so English can become a matter of 'doing' comprehension exercises:

The slithy toves gyred and gimbled in the wabe.
q. What kind of toves are they?
q. Where did they gyre and gimble?

— where all depends on syntax without meaning.

The experience of the curriculum is dominated not just by mathematics and English but by particular routines within the subjects. For children it is largely a matter of 'doing sums' or 'writing'. For this reason they yearn for more varied demands. They anticipate that in the more lavishly equipped secondary schools, with specialist rooms, they will be able to work in different ways, in experiments. They long to undertake tasks which give 'hands-on' experience, and contrast such practical work with what they see as endless writing. Against the associations of a certain amount of boredom with maths and English, children see science as a lively, practical activity. They like the idea of experiments, of testing phenomena and working on projects with each other. Children in primary schools relish the science they do and assume that secondary schools will provide many more experiences of this kind. What children like about science is the style, rather than the knowledge they accrue. It is the experimental way of working that they like, associating practical work not with technology but with science.

When children enter secondary schools they confirm the importance of experiments, as opposed to other kinds of work:

> 'The experiments in science. It's not all writing and writing and writing — but at least you have something to do and it's not writing and writing and writing all the time.' (boy, secondary)

> 'Well, you do things with Bunsen burners and different chemicals.' (girl, secondary)

The excitement children feel is the stronger for the contrast with the normal routines of the classroom. There is no mention of the significance of science. It is a small part of the given curriculum, but it offers the opportunity of doing something practical:

> 'You can make different things, study how things grow and blow up and evaporate in the air.' (boy, primary)

The limited amount of time given to science and technology underlines children's sense of pleasure in the subject. The attractions of the secondary school, with greater specialisms, are never so palpable as in science:

> 'You'll be doing lots of different experiments and things like that, like scientific experiments with different airs and gas. That will be totally different to what we do here but we are doing our science topic very soon.' (boy, primary)

Children do not see any of the maths work they do as experimental. For all the emphasis that is given to discovery methods by official reports, to the need for children to understand and develop principles, their actual experience is very different.[13] They never mention the possibility of exploring ideas in maths. Instead maths is writing by numbers. Nor do children associate any of the core curriculum with collaborative working. Their only collaboration appears to be with the textbooks or worksheets, and their rewards, the right answers. But in science they anticipate, and have some experience of working together to discover what happens when they conduct practical experiments:

> 'I'll like to do science because my brother tells me there is a very good science lab. with special scales and electric things there and we'll do all sorts of things with Mr ____. They have a lab. and it's properly laid out and they've got more expensive stuff there. . . .'
>
> (girl, primary)

Children's pleasure in science lies in the uses of equipment; in practical work:

> 'I like science because you do lots of interesting experiments.'
>
> (boy, secondary)

> 'I'd rather be doing science 'cos I like science. Because you have to do things, like wash and cleaning experiments.' (girl, secondary)

Science offers 'hands-on' experience and working with others. The pleasures it affords are not in the sense of purpose, but in the kinds of activity. Practical work is appreciated, and the only exceptions are those moments when something can go wrong. One girl feels clumsy:

> '. . . and I picked it up and dropped it all over the floor and I felt so stupid. I always do things like that and woodwork's like that. I'm afraid I'll cut or burn myself.' (girl, secondary)

Children appreciate different parts of the curriculum according to the amount of individual practical work they can carry out rather than according to the importance of the work. For this reason one other subject that is mentioned with as genuine appreciation as science is art. This subject also has the virtue of allowing children to *do* things, to produce results. It is carried out in a different environment and in ways which clearly contrast with the labour of maths and English. Like science, art seems to children a welcome break from the taxing work of the central curriculum:

153

> 'I love doing art because I can take my time over it and enjoy it more than anything else and I like to do something out of my head.'
>
> (girl, primary)

> 'My favourite lesson is art. Because we do a lot of painting and glueing. It's better than writing.' (boy, primary)

The pleasure in making, like the pleasure in experiments, is also carried through into the secondary school even if the nomenclature for the subject sometimes varies:

> 'Art . . . because I like drawing and messing about with paint and doing experiments with paints and things. I always do things at home like that . . .' (boy, secondary)

> 'Design, because I like making things and drawing and stuff like that.'
>
> (boy, secondary)

The appreciation of being able to do things with their hands as a relief from the purely cerebral is a theme which crosses curriculum boundaries, and which unites both those who are particularly good in certain areas and those who are not. The majority of children like to have a range of activities and to have time when they can enjoy making things. The sense of advantage that primary school children feel secondary schools contain derives from the idea of an extended curriculum; one that enters into new areas and new activities, together with specialist work places. But the pleasures in making things is also felt to be a mental pleasure; they like to 'do something out of their heads'.

The association of secondary schools with a wider curriculum also reveals itself in children's attitudes to modern languages. There is a sense of greater variety, of wider coverage of what should be known:

> 'They teach you more like German, French. When my brother went he didn't hardly know anything . . . I'll like French. I'd like to do French here. We do a bit of German. We do the days of the week.'
>
> (girl, primary)

Any extension of the curriculum seems to children interesting not when it is the product of a particular teacher's interests, but when they have personal curiosity about a subject that seems to connect with their own interests in the outside world:

'Well, I want to learn French. I'll like doing that. Because I've been to France. If I get the option I might do German because my brother's doing German.'   (girl, primary)

'I'd like to do French in the primary, so we might know a bit about it. I am in a way looking forward to that.'   (boy, primary)

Children show a hankering for new knowledge and different skills. The pleasure in what is new is also sustained in the secondary school. They know that learning a language is a practical advantage. But, as in many areas of the curriculum, certain things are learned which are not anticipated. As with foreign-language broadcasts, some children learn not only the language but associations of their own with the culture of that language:[14]

'French; I hate it because it's a different language, and some of the things they do in that country seem really soppy. Well, you know when they greet each other in the street, and that . . . and they kiss each other — really soppy.'   (boy, secondary)

In the HMI reports on the curriculum, despite their concern for a core, much is made of the need for doing more outside the central areas, especially in geography and history. But judging by the response of children these subjects have little impact in either primary or secondary schools. They are not new, like French, nor central like maths and English. They are not associated with activities, like art, nor with interesting experiments, like science. They remain just a small part of the work of schools; they are done up to a point, but in a way that does not strike the children as particularly salient. This is partly because they tend to be delivered through topic work and put under different, broad, labels and partly because the same topics, like Anglo-Saxons and Romans, seem to be repeated again and again:

'In humanities — I don't really like it. Too much of the same drawing and colouring in. We once did things about schools — like your mum and dad or gran went to, and you did about four or five different schools, but all in the same way. Ever so boring. Different years, but doing the same thing.'   (girl, secondary)

But then history is not a subject that is defined in their mind, since it is associated with craft activities — 'drawing and things like that' — and with broad topics. The lessons that children appreciate are those which suggest that they are learning something both relevant and interesing:

> '. . . like when we had to discuss who would survive on a desert island; how we were going to live and build a shelter.'   (girl, secondary)

They feel that there is something arbitrary about the choosing of topics and that the real study of geography and history will begin in the secondary school:

> 'It teaches you the basic things before you go on to the more complicated things like geography, physics. We don't do much geography in primary school. Just the basic work.'   (boy, primary)

But even the basic work provides difficulties of the kind that children do not find 'useful':

> 'Some things are useful in the primary but we do these weather charts with Miss . . . and they are dreadful they are. You have to do weather reports, weather charts. I hate them. You have to colour in the charts. I had quite a few fears about that because I got behind a lot.'
>
> (girl, primary)

Children at comprehensive schools hardly mention the humanities, either with approval or lack of it. It is clear that they do not make a strong impact, as if all the high expectations that children have, of doing 'real' work in specialist areas, are not fulfilled in the first year of secondary school. 'We just copy things all lesson' (girl, secondary). 'I can do it but it's boring' (boy, secondary).

Primary school children's anticipation of a curriculum that is broad and balanced is partly influenced by their desire for a variety of experiences. They hope that teaching styles will vary and that the curriculum will offer them new excitements. In all areas of the curriculum whether scientific or not, they hope for activities:

> 'I think it's about nature study, animals and things ... I ... we haven't been doing much nature work over the last few terms but there will be lots to do at the comp.'   (boy, primary)

'Well, I'd like to be able to go out of the school in lessons and find out about plants and everything, because I did that in one of the classes. You learn more because you can see all the things and you're allowed to take an insect book or a bird book or something, or an animal book.'   (girl, primary)

Children's interest in activity rather than the normal classroom routines also expresses itself in their interest in drama —

'I like drama, acting things, but that's not kind of hard work.'
                                                    (girl, secondary)

— also because it is in contrast to their normal style of learning:

'. . . you don't have to write.'   (boy, secondary)

In this way games are also seen as a contrast, and sometimes as a relief from classroom life, especially at secondary school where a variety of opportunities are on offer, from hockey, cricket and football to 'apparatus':

'Games. You don't have to do as much work and you don't have to use your brain as much because it gets tiring. You have to think hard. . . . You get all excited when you're changing to go out to rugby . . . it gets you in the mood for doing things properly.' (boy, secondary)

Children sometimes suggest that the activities that they least like are those which are 'academic'. But this should not be taken to imply that they are merely work-shy. Some of their greatest pleasures are with those parts of the curriculum, like English, in which they can be most creative. It is when they feel a sense of personal ownership of what they produce, when they have a sense of purpose, that they most enjoy using their minds. The contrasts are not between hard work and 'soft', but between activities they are engaged in and activities that are routine. A great deal of the curriculum is routine for children. They accept it and are used to it. But they long for greater demands and more variety, for different ways of work. The contrasts for children lie not so much in different subjects but in different ways of working:

'I like the doing better than the working.'   (boy, primary)

'Doing', for children, is an aspect of thinking, of creating something new. It is as if they had never quite forgotten the

157

intellectual pleasures of play, when making sense of the environment and their place in it and answering the question 'why' was a necessary everyday reality. But over that sharpened curiosity is spread a layer of routine. The normal experience of the curriculum is therefore quite dull. But children shrug their shoulders and accept what is given to them:

'To get a job you have to know English, science, history, maths and spellings.' (girl, secondary)

NOTES AND REFERENCES

1. Burgess, H. 'The primary curriculum: the example of mathematics.' In C. Cullingford, *The Primary Teacher*. London: Cassell, 1989, pp. 16–36.
2. Department of Education and Science (DES), *Primary Education in England*. London: HMSO, 1978.
3. DES, *The Curriculum 5–16* (Curriculum Matters 2). London: HMSO, 1985.
4. Entwistle, N. and Ramsden, P. *Understanding Student Learning*. London: Croom Helm, 1982.
5. Goodman, K. *Language and Literacy*, Vol. 1. Boston: Routledge and Kegan Paul, 1982. Smith, F. *Understanding Reading*. New York: Holt, Rinehart and Winston, 1971.
6. White, R. with Brockington, D. *Tales out of School: Consumers' Views of British Education*. London: Routledge and Kegan Paul, 1983.
7. Thomas, N. 'Class teaching and curriculum support.' In Cullingford, *op. cit.*, pp. 37–55.
8. The 'Great Debate' which followed Prime Minister Callaghan's Ruskin College speech in 1976.
9. Galton, M., Simon, B. and Croll, P. *Inside the Primary Classroom*. London: Routledge and Kegan Paul, 1980.
10. DES, 1978, *op. cit.*
11. Burgess, *op. cit.*
12. Söter, A. 'Recent research on writing: implications for writing across the curriculum.' *Journal of Curriculum Studies* **19** (5), 425–438, 1987.
13. Eg. the Cockcroft report. DES, *Mathematics Counts*. London: HMSO, 1982.
14. Belson, W. *The Impact of Television: Methods and Findings in Television Research*. London: Crosby Lockwood, 1967.

CHAPTER 10
The Purpose of Schools

'Really you need to go to school to get a job when you're older.'
(girl, primary)

Children go to school because they have to. It is part of the preordained experience, divided between hours spent in one way at home and another way at school. Very rarely, if ever, is the purpose of school discussed with children. They go to school without deeply questioning why they do. There is such a laconic air of acceptance that those who do have doubts, and play truant, are considered deviant by the children as well as the teachers. The way that children approach their work, accepting the given curriculum, submitting to the rules, is one symptom of how unquestioned the whole process of schooling has become. It also means that children do not necessarily go to school with a sense of personal fulfilment, or individual curiosity. School is a part of life with its own demands and traumas.

Discussing the purpose of schools is not a part of the curriculum, either. Teachers simply do not spend time engaged in delineating why things need to be learned. The many analyses of what should be in the curriculum, broad and balanced, physical and spiritual, all suggest that there are many things that children need to know, for future citizenship and well-being. But even if there is a consensus of what the curriculum should be, such a sense of purpose is not conveyed to children. The lack of such analysis marks out both the whole school experience and the individual pieces of work that children undertake. And in this hiatus, the influence of parents and the community becomes the more strong.

Teachers are busily submerged in the day-to-day problems of the school. They are delivering a given curriculum with a huge apparatus of assessment procedures. They are therefore spending exhausting hours keeping up with the marking and the classroom organization, making sure that attainment targets are met. They, too, are under scrutiny and share with the children in their class the burden of outside expectations. They, too, submit to school.

This leaves little time or energy for shared reflection. It is as if schools had become a conspiracy of submission.

And yet teachers have their own sense of purpose, even if it can be in conflict with the demands made on them by local authorities, the government or parents. They might be inarticulate about their own missionary tendencies, or realize that to be so well-meaning is out of fashion, but they do have a more subtle idea of their role, and the important matters of what children learn, than a mere delivery of the curriculum. They know those moments when they and the children share a new discovery. Children glimpse a greater sense of purpose when they see the relevance of what they are doing, and when they see the connection between what they are learning and their own lives. But the freedom of manoeuvre in any national curriculum, through its weight of assessment, is limited, and the curriculum is approached not so much in a spirit of discovery as with a sense of awe. There is so much that must be learned.

Teachers are aware that children are learning things other than the formal curriculum. In Great Britain in particular, there is less distinction between the pastoral role of the teacher and the academic role. The tradition of the teacher as being *in loco parentis* is strong. Social values are being presented by the school as well as the parents. In France and Germany the teacher presents what is to be learned; it is the parents who are deemed to be responsible for discipline.[1] But in Great Britain teachers present a strong case for their responsibility for the behaviour of their pupils.[2] Whilst this places particular demands on the role of teachers it is reflected not only in social expectations but in their sense of the purpose of schools.[3] When teachers analyse their roles they draw attention to the importance of behaviour. When they talk to the children about their expectations they will also almost invariably concentrate on how children should behave. All moral messages are centred on the same theme.[4]

When teachers are questioned about their own aims in teaching they present a picture of their schools as microcosms of society, in which children are learning to adapt to the behaviour of others, and learning to fulfil social roles. In interviews about the purpose of schooling, teachers lean heavily on the social aspects of school.[5] They do not labour the point about

160

competition or qualifications, despite the pressure on them to do as well, if not better, than other neighbouring schools. They do not stress academic outcomes, or their own particular interests. Instead they talk at length about the pupil's needs in terms of 'coping' with social pressures both within and outside school. They use the word 'autonomy' as a symbol of the individual child's ability to work out his own solutions, to be adaptable and nurture his self-belief. Teachers stress more than the 'academic'. They want children to be 'self-reliant', and 'in charge of themselves'. They express concern with the 'autonomy of the individual' and the 'courage to stick up for things they believe are right' without saying what these should be. They understand their role to be engaged in bringing out the individuality of each pupil, 'in asking them to make decisions and to develop some degree of self-control and self-discipline'.

> 'I think really my main objective is giving the children first of all a feeling of warmth and serenity, umm, a nice cosy atmosphere in which to work, and love. That's the basis of what I try to do . . . and once you've got those things you can start linking on to them the basic things they need to go through life — not only basic skills, but skills in connecting with other people, social skills . . .'

Teachers stress the social aspects of education far more strongly than the purpose of what children learn. It is as if knowledge were a by-product of individual peace of mind, as if social development automatically led to greater motivation so that children would then wish to learn. The purpose of different subjects, from history to mathematics, from content to skills, is left relatively unexplored. If the children are happy in the classroom and seem to be engaged in what they are doing, that seems to be enough. If children behave well, and understand all the organizational signals that come their way, that appears to be the crucial point of school.

Nothing could contrast more with the attitudes of parents. The purpose of school may be primarily social to teachers. When parents are interviewed about how *they* they see the purpose of school, they show both a single-minded concern with the success of their own children and a clear sense of how this success is to be achieved.[6] They want to have the experience of seeing their

161

children do so well at examinations that they gain the qualifications necessary to a good job. They express their ambition in pragmatic terms:

> 'I want them to have a better education so they can get a better job than what I've done.'

Whereas teachers only rarely mention exams and never talk about the job market, parents see jobs as the primary concern for education. They express this as a 'better chance in life', or 'something to fall back on'. They talk about their 'ambition for their child' and their fear of their child's inability to find employment:

> 'They could take not necessarily the top exams and get some form of qualifications at the end of their schooling, so when they leave school they can at least start making their way in the world and make a living and not sort of end up having to be stuck on the dole and not having no qualifications and having to struggle then for the rest of their life.'

In any education system there is bound to be some tension between the needs of the individual and the needs of society as a whole, between personal self-development and the teaching of specific skills. Whatever the state of the economy, the government is concerned with the creation of a highly trained work-force, with the skills necessary to support industrial society. The government tends to see itself, in discussions about educational outcomes, as representing the views of parents. To the extent of being concerned with the job market and the skills necessary for securing jobs, it has some justification for doing so. The government may have a general view about qualified manpower, and the parent a particular concern for the success of his or her own children in winning jobs, but both see schools as giving children the best preparation for profitable employment. There is an obvious tension between individual and social needs, and some ambiguity between personal knowledge and the ability to perform well in employment, but an underlying agreement seems to exist amongst those outside the educational system itself.

For children, like their parents, there is little ambiguity about the purpose of schools. Children in primary and secondary schools express their beliefs in a variety of ways but about one matter they are, without exception, agreed. The purpose of schools is to prepare them for jobs. By the time children approach the end of their primary school career, the purpose of schools seems to them obvious. This underlying sense of purpose provides a coherence that makes sense of all the different experiences they undergo; all the routine work and the waiting. It makes them assume that there must be a pragmatic purpose in the curriculum, even if teachers do not say anything about what the purpose is. Primary children return repeatedly to the same theme:

'If I didn't go to school I'd know nothing and wouldn't be able to get a job or nothing.' (boy)

'I come to get a good job.' (girl)

'It's for teaching you to make sure you get a good job when you leave.' (boy)

'If you want to get a job . . . it might help me with my job. It's important 'cos it helps to get jobs.' (girl)

There is no evidence to suggest that teachers ever mention employment. They do not praise employment nor cajole children into working by pointing out the consequences of not doing so.

The pervasive sense of the importance of access to jobs is well established in primary school children. They already share, with their parents, a view on the long-term outcomes of school:

'When you need a job and you hadn't been to school, it would be hard to get a job. . . . Really you need to go to school to get a job when you're older.' (girl)

Primary school children are faced with the fundamental change of style that will confront them when they pass on to a secondary school. In many ways they are in awe of the secondary school, because primary school is viewed as a passing phase before they go on to more serious business. But secondary schools are more serious because they are closer to the world of work. Once they start secondary school, children's sense of the purpose of schools is confirmed:

'If you didn't [come to school] you wouldn't learn anything — you wouldn't get any jobs.' (girl)

'To learn — to be able to get a job. You got to be able to spell and add.' (boy)

'It's for teaching children how to learn, like maths and sums so when they grow up they won't start going round without any job, and being unemployed.' (girl)

'To help get an education — when you're older to get a job and things.'

'Getting an education', which includes the basic skills, is commensurate with 'getting a job' rather than learning more subtle social skills. Success in school is seen in terms of the outcome, in terms of subsequent achievement.

Children's view of the purpose of schooling pervades many of their attitudes — towards the curriculum, towards teachers and towards discipline. They see school as a kind of preparation rather than as a complete experience in itself. Whilst they might seem to accept the curriculum that is presented to them, they do so on the assumption that it has the underlying purpose of preparing them for employment, preparation that is more obvious in some subjects than in others. They concur with their parents that what they do should be relevant, even when accepting that some of the activities they experience, like drama, do not have an obvious application in terms of knowledge. The skills they learn are seen to be relevant to later experiences, whether in some obscure way related to jobs they will do or in the ability to deal with daily events.

It is only after they have left school that children articulate their bewilderment at some of the 'irrelevancies' they underwent there. Whilst at school, the purpose is so unexplored that they rarely question what they are doing. Subsequently, especially amongst the unemployed, there appears to be real bewilderment about why the purpose of school was left so disappointingly unclear, a natural reaction to their years of belief that the acquisition of jobs was what schools were eventually concerned with.[7] It is clear that children were not given any alternative vision of the purpose of school. They all stick to the belief that the purpose of school is preparation for jobs. This belief begins in primary schools.

Children's understanding of the underlying purpose of school manifests itself in many ways. They make the assumption that the skills they learn must have a direct bearing on the kinds of work they will do in employment. 'When I grow up I want to be a speller.' They accept that learning tables, reading and writing are all geared towards one ultimate end, even if it is not particularly apparent at the time:

> 'I suppose learning your tables could help you get a job.'
> (boy, primary)

> 'When you leave school and you're older and you can get a job, you'll know how to read and write and you'll know English and maths and all that lot.'
> (girl, primary)

Children accept that the curriculum given to them is divided into tasks and knowledge. There are skills they must acquire and subjects they must take. Reading and writing are seen in terms of 'learning to get a good job' as if there were a utilitarian end in everything presented to them. At school they do not question the connections between the immediate and ultimate purposes. Some parts of the curriculum might be obvious in this way:

> 'It can help you get a job again because . . . like maths can help you get into computers.'
> (girl, secondary)

But every part of the curriculum is ultimately connected to the job market:

> 'To learn about things, and history and science and that, so that when you come out you'll be able to get a decent job.'   (boy, secondary)

Thus children interpret the unexplored purposes in the curriculum.

In the connection between the curriculum and jobs, examinations play a central role. On one level the curriculum that is presented to them is obviously 'relevant' because it is made up of the subjects that form the examinations. Childen take the idea of qualifications seriously and recognize the importance of examinations long before they take them, as the real end of their learning. They might 'drop out' of the competition when

165

they are confronted by the actual 16+ examinations, but at primary school and in their first year at secondary school, children are unambiguous about the importance of examinations. They assume that they cannot gain good employment without qualifications of the traditional sort:

> 'Learning so that when you grow up you'll learn how to find a job and add up things that are quite hard. It's for exams.'   (girl, primary)

> 'If I didn't go to school I'd know nothing and wouldn't be able to get a job or nothing. It's really for people to learn things you didn't know before and when you are older you'll have so many GCSEs you can get what you want. If you didn't go to school you wouldn't have no GCSEs and you wouldn't ever get a job nowhere.'   (boy, primary)

The skills that are learned are all learned so that they can be tested:

> 'Exams see how good you are on your tables, English, maths and that . . .'   (boy, primary)

And the thought of leaving the school at sixteen to get a job pervades the answers of children in primary schools:

> 'When you're about 16 you do your exams and then leave school and try to get a job.'   (girl, primary)

Primary school children's analysis of the purpose of school suggests that there is a natural progression towards leaving qualifications and that therefore schooling becomes more and more serious as they go through it. Such an assumption about the greater importance of secondary schools is confirmed by those in them:

> 'Primary school was an introductory period to what you're going to be doing up here because we don't do handwriting or anything up here . . .'   (boy, secondary)

> 'It's to learn things so that when you grow up you get a good education. The secondary school is for a good education. You wouldn't know anything if you didn't go to school and you wouldn't get a job.'   (girl, secondary)

By the time they reach secondary school the importance of doing well in examinations looms larger. By then children see the importance of this so clearly that they feel the power that the school has over them, as if the school were somehow responsible for 'placing' them in jobs. For some children it is obviously success at exams that counts:

> 'It is when you get older and you need your A levels and your GCSEs.' (boy, secondary)

> 'The GCSEs are important because if you don't get any you won't get a job or anything, and you'll just be on your own, nowhere really.' (girl, secondary)

But many children assume that the school is not only responsible for preparing them for exams but a central agent in reporting on them, in making sure that if they work hard they will ultimately be rewarded:

> 'It depends on the report you get at school to see if you can get a job or not.' (boy, secondary)

> 'The comp. tell you what kind of jobs you're fit for. If you want to get a good job you've got to really work hard at the comp. That's the kind of second step to being an adult and just before you finish they tell you what job you're qualified for, and then you can choose one of them. You're qualified when you learn most of your subjects and you've got GCSEs and A levels.' (girl, primary)

Children reflect a 'top-down' model of the curriculum. All is dictated by outcome. The importance of qualifications is the more powerful in children's minds because of their awareness of unemployment. Children hold few illusions about the job market and appear to sense the competition for those jobs which are available. Like their parents they are quick to fear the possibility of being on the dole:

> 'Well, with today's unemployment you need so many GCSEs and A levels and degrees as you can get and the only way you can get these is to go to school.' (boy, primary)

> 'Later in our life we would want to get a job and not hang around on the dole and we could have GCSEs and A levels and get good qualifications ... it does prepare you for some jobs. If you forget everything your life is a misery and you wouldn't be able to have a job or anything.' (girl, primary)

167

Whilst children reiterate the importance of qualifications, they are also concerned that they should manifest the kinds of ability that would attract employers. They realize that some of these abilities are the skills they will have learned, like tables and spelling. But they also know that the way they present themselves is important. Like their parents, they see a connection between the social abilities learned in the school and employability. Although teachers tend to stress social ability rather than jobs, and parents insist on the importance of qualifications and jobs rather than a child's 'autonomy', children see the connection between the two. Both help them in getting a job:

> 'Teaching us what we might need to know when we get a job: how to be neat and have manners and how to behave properly.'
>
> (girl, primary)

> 'Well, we have to come. It's to teach you things. Manners and that. It does prepare you for some jobs.' (boy, primary)

The hidden curriculum of the school — the implicit understanding of certain codes of behaviour — has a major role to play in children's understanding of the purpose of education. They realize that *how* they present themselves is as important as what they present, that knowledge is more than a series of learned facts. The tension between 'knowing that' and 'knowing how' is always before them.[8] They know that there are other dimensions to the accumulation of knowledge:

> 'So that if you have children then you can tell them how to get a job and everything. To know things if anyone asks you.' (boy, primary)

Children agree that the prime motivation of school is to pass exams for the sake of employability. They also know that there are other skills they must learn. *Not* to have a job has fearful consequences, but it is also embarrassing. The children feel that knowing how to behave, and doing well at school, is significant because otherwise they would feel silly or incapable. The idea of the interview — the combination of knowledge and presentation — is symbolic of the intended outcome of school in children' eyes. It suggests children's desire to possess the capacity to perform in given social circumstances. After all, the ability to deal with various circumstances derives from being able to deal with formal demands:

> 'Because if you don't do it, you won't get a job . . . and they give you kinds of things and say what kind of bus you go on and all that and if you don't know they won't give you a job.'　　(girl, secondary)

Whilst children recognize that the subjects given them are examinable and part of the central route of qualifications, they also acknowledge that they are learning other skills; those that teachers delineate as 'social'. The difference is that whilst teachers value social autonomy for its own sake, children wish to acquire social skills so that they can impress would-be employers. They wish to know how to handle themselves in the wider world. They also express some unease that what they are learning in school is not necessarily relevant to such circumstances.

Children also fear embarrassment. They crave knowing how to manipulate social events, from shopping to being interviewed, because they recognize how easy it is to make mistakes. They learn embarrassment because of the difficulties they can have in school:

> 'It's important because you want to get it right and nothing wrong and you want to impress the teacher and things like that.'
> 　　　　　　　　　　　　　　　　　　　　　　(girl, secondary)

Teachers are not the only people who children feel would be critical of any lack of knowledge. They are aware of the wider social world, where the ability to count or read forms makes some sense of what they learned in school:

> 'If you didn't do the work you wouldn't have no education at all and you would just go around dumb and not be able to write when you leave school.'　　　　　　　　　　　　　　　　(girl, secondary)

> 'Helping you to learn because if you didn't have school and someone said "What's one and one", if you didn't have school you'd just stay at home all the time and get really bored.'　　(boy, secondary)

> 'Someone might make fun of you when you're older if you're not good at maths of something.'　　　　　　　　　　　　(boy, primary)

Children see schools in their wider social context. Although the school may seem a complete world in itself, with its own rules and hierarchies, children are constantly aware of the pressures of the outside world. The sense of excitement in learning that pervades the very first experiences of school is replaced by a more pragmatic attitude, when children separate ability and hard work. By the time they are ten, however, they feel the pressure to do well very powerfully, either out of determination — 'you've got to do it or you'll never learn' (girl, secondary) — or out of fear of the consequences — 'so we don't get into trouble and all that' (boy, secondary). The one purpose that pervades all their thinking is the practical one that 'if you stick it hard at school so you'll get a good job' (girl, primary). To a physically handicapped child the need to get a job is just as important:

'My wife will be working. I don't want to be unemployed. I want to have money so that I can keep all the electronic stuff in my house going — and another thing — to keep all my electric stuff for lifting me and things. If I don't get a good job, I can't afford that.'

(boy, secondary)

Children find schools complex places. Their analysis of teaching and learning styles, and their awareness of schools as purveyors of a set of rules as well as social centres, demonstrates that. But schools are the more complex in their eyes because of two factors. The first is that many of the assumptions about the purpose of schools, presented through the hidden curriculum, are rarely made explicit, so that children hold on to the idea of the ultimate purpose of schools in a way that seems to be despite, rather than because of, what they are told. The second factor is that if the underlying purpose of school is ultimately preparation for jobs, then the school is further complicated by having an ambiguous relationship to the world outside. The sense of disappointment that children feel after they have left school is not just with the lack of availability of jobs but because of their sense that the school appeared unconcerned with the lives of children in the adult world. It is as if the pupils were trying to make sense of the complexities by assuming that all they did, the styles of learning and the curriculum presented to them, led to the same end. What is certain is that the real purpose of schools as preparation for employment pervades their notions of all that goes on within schools.

In these attitudes children remain strongly influenced by their homes and their peer groups. It is as if the world of school were disconnected from the world outside. The central values of the job market are not just an indication of children's pragmatism. They demonstrate how little energy is spent within schools on justifying what they are doing. The curriculum is presented without analysis. The purposes of learning are left implicit. Children therefore have to make sense of what goes on in their own terms, as if they remain outsiders looking in, rather than being closely involved in school.

Schools remain the worlds of teachers in which children are temporary guests. Children recognize that there are certain given factors to which they must succumb. There is a given curriculum and a given set of rules. Against this the school is a social centre in which children can discuss all the issues that are not formally addressed. In these circumstances it is not surprising that children should look back on their experience of school with some puzzlement. They do not see what goes on in school as having a sense of purpose, or as being relevant. Whilst at school children *assume* that what they do has some kind of connection to the world outside. Afterwards they are disabused.

The world of work, presented to children at home, and the world of school, are like two cultures, side by side. Sometimes the world of work absorbs them the more and causes conflict. Those who help on farms or work on fairgrounds begin to scrutinize their school experience in a different way:

> 'I often get fed up and bored. . . . I'd rather be at my grandad's on the farm, feeding the chickens and driving the tractor.'   (boy, primary)

For these children it is the parents who have to cajole them into work, reiterating the need for qualifications for long-term job security.

> 'I want to finish school and get to work but my mum says you really need to go to college to be a farmer.'   (boy, primary)

For all the children the kind of belief that their parents have in their future prospects drives them back to school:

> 'My mum says I've got to start pulling myself together.'

171

'My dad says a good job's where you get a lot of money.'

In the end it is this which defines the purpose of schooling.

NOTES AND REFERENCES

1. Broadfoot, P. and Osborn, M. with M. Gilly and A. Paillet. 'Teachers' conceptions of their professional responsibility: some international comparisons.' *Comparative Education* **23** (3), 287–302, 1987.
2. Department of Education and Science (DES) *Discipline in Schools. Report of the Committee of Enquiry chaired by Lord Elton.* London: HMSO, 1989.
3. Concern with classroom violence, and the need for teachers to learn how to overcome it, seems to be a particularly British as opposed to European phenomenon, as if the social expectations are remarkably different.
4. Sharp, R. and Green A. *Education and Social Control.* London: Routledge and Kegan Paul, 1975.
5. Cullingford, C. *Parents, Teachers and Schools.* London: Robert Royce, 1985, pp. 140–142.
6. *Ibid.*, pp. 135–138.
7. White, R. with Brockington, D. *Tales out of School: Consumers' Views of British Education.* London: Routledge and Kegan Paul, 1983.
8. Cf. Goodnow, J. and Burns, A. *Home and School: A Child's Eye View.* London: Allen and Unwin, 1985.

CHAPTER 11

Conclusions: The Inner World of Children

'Beautiful moments . . . terrible half hours.'
(Contemporary critic on Wagner's *Tristan and Isolde*)

Children are naturally adaptable. Even their earliest experience
forces them to respond to their surroundings, as well as to try to
manipulate them. When the time comes they accept the existence
of schools, since no one questions it, and they learn how to cope
with the peculiar demands, excitements and tensions that schools
provide. Children so readily accept that they have to go to school
that they do not question many obscure regulations or difficult
experiences. At one level children are positive about school and
only later, when they have left, do they begin to articulate their
wonder about the purpose of what they had to undergo. But this
more questioning attitude towards schools is already being
developed by those within them. At one level children accept the
rules, the curriculum and the organization of school as it is. At
another level their experience of schools as institutions is more
complex.

Those parts of school that children most appreciate are not
always the most formal ones. They like good lessons, well
presented with interesting experiments — lessons which demand
something active from them. But they are also accustomed to
work that seems to be designed to fill time. They appreciate good
explanations from teachers, but know they learn from each other.
They accept the need to jostle from classroom to classroom, but
express a strong desire for peace. Between moments of
excitement, mostly with their friends, whether in the classroom
or outside, there is also a considerable amount of anguish.
Naturally the picture that emerges is complex, but it is not the
picture that is normally presented of schools.

Children as well as teachers do their best in often difficult
circumstances. They are adaptable and cheerful even about some
of the difficulties that schools present. But the question remains
whether the circumstances are the most appropriate for
children's learning and development. One of the fundamental

173

truths that children's analysis brings out is whether the best use is made of children's capacities when so much of their emotional energy seems to be spent in overcoming difficulties. Schools are unusual institutions and whilst children acknowledge their necessity and their ultimate purpose in preparing them for jobs, they subsequently question whether they have really been fulfilled by the experience. Schools are, after all, potential battlegrounds, not only between peer groups but between children and staff, to the extent that a power struggle can take place in what Measor and Woods witnessed as an 'attempted coup' by pupils.[1] If we take what children are saying seriously it suggests questioning many habits that we, as teachers, have taken for granted.

There is always a gap between children's capacities and their actual performance in schools. Children's capacities for understanding and thoughtfulness about crucial questions is both deeper and begins far earlier than some educational theorists have recognized. Many of the essential concerns of very young children are those which remain the most significant for the rest of our lives; the meaning of life and death; the question of relationships with other people; the individual in society. But it appears that most children address these issues with each other, and that they are not a central part of the formal curriculum of school. And yet children begin their exploration of the world and their emotions very young. By eighteen months they already show understanding of themselves and others in the experience and communication of emotions.[2] The earliest significant help they receive is from their parents and others long before they come to school. It is acknowledged that the pre-school years are essential to children's development. It is not always so clear that a greater connection could be made between what children are learning in their personal experience and what they could be learning in school.

Children's performance in schools depends on their attitudes. Those who are highly motivated and whose curiosity has been encouraged are those who are able to make sense of the tasks presented to them. Learning depends on children's ability to concentrate and to pay attention.[3] And yet the children interviewed signify that they do not feel that the demands that are put on them need particular attention of the kind that is self-directed. They rarely suggest there is a reason for learning particular parts of the curriculum beyond the general preparation for employment. It is as if some of the key motivations of learning — the desire to understand and relate knowledge to personal experience — were being left out. As a result children tend to pick up moral attitudes and ideals from each other, boys in their peer groups and girls in theirs.[4]

For children the school is a social centre where they have the opportunity to meet others and explore friendships. They accept the outer purpose of school, as their parents do, as a means to enable them to compete for jobs. But they know that the inner purpose has much more to do with testing relationships with others, either singly or in groups. They do not, as the teachers do, assume that the school is there to teach them social values, or the ability to be both autonomous and concerned with other people.[5] Instead they explore their changing relationships with others as a form of self-exploration, using others to test out their ideas. Many of the attitudes children derive from their school experience are a result of wide-ranging discussions with their peer groups. They try out ideas. They pursue discoverable truths. They accept that they can change and learn new things just as inexorably as they change friends.[6] Many of the moral issues that concern children appear to be left to the children to talk about with each other.

Children appreciate the value of friends as teachers, as well as people with whom to discuss important or trivial issues. The potential for using children to help each other, where they show great patience and understanding of learning difficulties as well as learning how to care for and adapt to others, has very rarely been taken up, although it is often recognized.[7] It is clear that in the changing patterns of friendship children feel the need to do more than have a comfortable partner. They use friends as a challenge, and are quick to recognize who can help them and who cannot. To this extent their attitude to friendship is functional. They expect change, and expect intense discussion, just as much as they expect trust. Children need relationships not just for security but for self-exploration, for learning about their own sense of identity and what they learn about their values.[8]

One of the subjects about which children talk to each other reveals both the way that children observe what goes on in schools and how schools do not address the issues directly. It stems from children's exploration of relationships, with each other and with the teachers. The subject is the nature of power, whether derived from age or from position, and the nature of influence. Children are concerned with the broader aspects of politics, although they would not label their discussions with this term since they associate 'politics' with party political diatribes on television. For many people, including voters in democracies, politics seems to be a subject of complete indifference. They associate it with the propaganda of political parties and with the dishonesty of politicians. Any suggestion that people might have a close interest in it seems absurd, even though they are directly affected by political decisions. This lack of interest in the wide aspects of politics is also assumed to be the lot of schoolchildren, partly because they are supposed to be incapable of understanding the niceties of society and partly because the politicians fear that their rivals might use politics as a means for propaganda if it were part of the curriculum. Given the association of politics with the statements of party political broadcasts, it is not surprising that a more old-fashioned view of politics as a matter of common everyday interest is not easily encouraged. And yet children witness politics, both in the school and on the television every day.

Although children are deemed to have little interest in politics, they all express politicial views, and learn their political attitudes just at a time when little ostensible attention is given to them. Although children are not encouraged to be aware of this, they are learning from their parents, from their friends, from their views of what they see on television, if not from television itself, and from the example of school. They learn about power and authority and the ways in which human beings organize themselves, which is the stuff of politics. No one can escape the consequences of the need for the translation of social action into a means of control and organization. Children are as capable as the indifferent voter of having political insights. Their early grasp of the complexities of human relationships, and their understanding of the contrasting organizations in which they are placed, implies a curiosity about the ways in which social groups cohere, which for them is a necessity rather than a luxury. Schools continually remind them of the importance of rules.

Children's views of politics are derived from home and naturally reflect many of their parents' attitudes and degree of knowledge. But they all share common assumptions about politics. One is that the world contains certain high authorities who are powerful and rightly so. Children do not say that they are always right but that they are to be obeyed. Children do not always make a distinction between real power (a president or prime minister) and ostensible power (the Queen) but they accept the idea of power none the less. They also believe that the rule of law is absolute. They do not also assume that is is always fair, but they feel it is inevitable. Children's underlying view of political structures is that there is a clear hierarchy of power; that the politicians generally try to do good but that even if they don't they retain the authority of power. This does not imply that children are optimistic, or that they think the world is inexorably improving. On the contrary many children state that the world is getting steadily worse rather than better. But they still accept the static nature of political structures and the domination of a few important figures.

Children's views on authority bring out the contrast between the two levels of school, the formal and the informal. They see a need for rigid structures, but within those structures explore a number of alternatives. What is interesting about children's perception of the power and authority of school is that it rarely gives any hint of any moral perspectives. Children assume that the rules exist because otherwise it would be impossible to manage. Rules exist because people are naturally bad rather than because they need to be taught what is good. Children's views of discipline are pragmatic rather than moral, and it would be no surprise if there were a close connection between children's experience of actual social organizations, like school, and their views on other, larger, social structures. But it is difficult to detect in children's attitudes any attempt to make them think of underlying moral issues, or explorations of the purpose of education. Teachers very rarely have an opportunity to discuss the purpose of schools with each other or with the children. The time is taken up with the tasks of teaching, keeping up with meeting constant demands of the curriculum in what is one of the most demanding jobs in the world. But children want to be reminded of the important questions. They do not want to reserve discussion of the purposes of life to the subculture of peer groups and discussions with friends, when the exploration of attitudes depends so much on shared mythologies. The evidence that emerges from these interviews suggests that children feel a need to talk about the purpose of what they are learning. They fall back on the idea of employability not only because they are pragmatic, or because this view is socially pervasive, or held by their parents, but also for want of anything better. One implication for teachers is that more attention could be paid to discussing with children what schools are for.

Children's sense of the supreme importance of the job market has other implications for teachers. Some might think that the education system has done itself a grave disservice by gaining the reputation of being a supplier of qualifications, so that the successful ones will be amply rewarded. At a time of high unemployment, schools cannot depend on this assumption alone, even if very many of them would anyway want to. But children do see schools in terms of competition, whether some deliberately drop out or others are determined to make a success of it, whether they fear failure or are confident of success. The question is whether teachers can make more use of these attitudes, not by being narrower in their own interpretation of what takes place in school as in a mechanistic 'core' curriculum, but through exploring the purposes of the curriculum more deeply. At the moment there seems to be a clear dichotomy between children's and teacher's attitudes towards school, and this dichotomy is of benefit to neither one nor the other.

The statements children make about school have many implications for the way that schools are run and the way they are resourced. On many issues that concern the general government of school children express important insights. No account of the curriculum, whether of the 'core' or of the other subjects, can sensibly leave out the experience that children undergo, and how they understand the distinction between the processes of what they are learning and the body of knowledge.

The whole debate about the relationship between the school and its community, and between the curriculum and its social context, is addressed by what the children say, in their attempts to balance different influences and their desire to place schools in a larger, as well as more personal, world. Children draw attention both to their preferred styles of working and to their insight into what makes a successful lesson. They are equally clear about what kind of teaching seems to them unsuccessful. What children are exploring has implications for the whole ethos of school.

Many isssues that these children have raised need to be addressed. Some make one wonder about the nature of schooling itself, both in terms of schools as institutions and in terms of their relationship to the world in which they are placed. But other issues affect the schools themselves. Are the purposes of education explained? Do children feel comfortable in school? Do they feel fully involved in what they are doing? Do they get the best out of each other? Is there a sufficient variety of teaching styles? Many of these questions are not new. But they are given resonance by the evidence that children put before us.

One of the central questions that children have to address is the nature and content of the curriculum. The debates about content and the boundaries between subjects[9] seem to leave children out. This is a pity. Children wish to make sense of what they are learning, and yet much of the curriculum presented to them is left unexplained. Children might not question what teachers give them at the time, but they do later. The desire for a relevant curriculum is not, however, confined to those who have left school.

Children interviewed by Goodnow and Burns expressed a desire for more 'relevant' knowledge and for a change in the curriculum to accommodate this.[10] They felt that they should be taught more about *how* to do things rather than knowing *about* things. They wanted many more links between school and the 'real' world. Children expressed a desire to be prepared for jobs, and for understanding the world in which they would have to work. They wanted to understand the context in which they lived, and how to adapt themselves to the context of home and work as well as school.[11]

Within schools children express a universal desire for a greater sense of purpose. Sometimes this emerges in discussions about a particular part of the curriculum. English is one subject in which sixteen-year-olds find a contradiction between what they perceive as the teachers' ideas of grammar and 'correctness' and their own desire to view the subject as professional preparation, with a strong underlying purpose to this end.[12] Many children feel that the schools do not ally themselves closely with their own needs or aspirations. Whilst they assume that the school shares many of their values, they do consequently wonder why so many of their actions are constrained, as if there were a contradiction between the expressed values and the actual ones.[13] Children express pragmatic attitudes towards school, not exaggerating the dichotomy between their own values and the society in which they are placed but finding few reciprocal echoes in the institutions. They do not view themselves, at fifteen, as undergoing particular storm and stress, but are concerned with central matters like getting a job on the one hand, and enjoying their lives on the other.[14]

For pupils the 'hidden' curriculum is as important as the formal. This means that what schools present to them has a somewhat oblique relationship with the rest of their lives. The existence or absence of 'child-centredness' is not particularly noticed by the children when the social skills they are learning are those to do with understanding social systems and they know to what extent they need to conform. To understand the experience of children in schools we need to know that schools are not in themselves central to their existence. The very formalities of school leave the individual alone and private. It is partly for this reason that children appreciate the need for discipline. It might also reveal a particular attitude to human nature, but discipline is seen as the imposition of a social order into which they need to fit, and in which they can go their own way. Even something as unhidden as the reasons for social discipline appear unexplored.

In the framework of rules children find it easy to avoid learning. Even when they are engaged in a task, as in 'time on task', they find that much of what they do is routine. Being seen to be busy can be as important as doing work. Guessing what the teacher wants, which includes quiet attention to the task in hand, can be as significant as new discoveries. And yet children appreciate the formality and purpose of their actual work. They do not necessarily prefer any lack of demands. They therefore appreciate not only those teachers who bring a variety of explanations and examples to bear, but those who have high expectations of their pupils. The problem for teachers, given the resources at their command, is that it is very difficult to fulfil the ideal of making proper demands on children.

Schools belong to teachers rather than children. This is the way they have been designed, and this is the way that both parents and governments see them. This separation of the institution from the world outside is both an experience for those in them and a collective memory. The views of children in school are close to those who have left. Once children have left school such negative attitudes come to the fore very quickly. White and Brockington, for example, interviewed young men and women aged between sixteen and twenty-three who had left school and were mostly unemployed.[15] They found that their memories, of primary as well as secondary schools, and about transfer from one to the other, were vivid. They found that all the pupils felt that their own schooling lacked relevance and purpose. The curriculum was felt to be irrelevant to their subsequent lives. Looking back, the pupils wished that what they had learned had been directed towards the skills they found they needed. Even more tellingly, they felt that schools did not address issues in the political and social environment in which they lived. They wished schools had presented a more relevant sense of purpose.

In school children both look for a sense of purpose and accept what they are given. Their acceptance of schools as they are means that they have a natural pragmatism about their experience. They might share the negative views of their elders, and dwell on some of the difficult experiences they undergo, but they are not just negative about school. They appreciate what is good and what individual teachers are trying to do. They accept the need for rules and discipline. But there appears to be a gap between their private experience of school and the school's implied sense of purpose. This comes about partly because schools rarely advertise their purpose to the pupils themselves.

The question of 'relevance' seems to be a vacuum filled by general *social* attitudes towards school. In this way children are conservative and express opinions about school which are far closer to the declaration of governments and civil servants than are the statements of teachers.

If children express conservative attitudes to the purpose of schools, to the curriculum and to discipline, they also show a feeling for liberal *practices*, for a greater degree of self-help, flexible means of working and for different teaching styles. This is not just a question of different levels of perception, between the outer control and the inner testing of such control, but one which is unified in children's minds by the question of purposes, of the need to pursue *why* they are undertaking certain tasks. The children are trying to find a unity in their own personal experience in which all the contradictory parts of this experience make sense. They wish to understand how to make the best of friends in work as well as play, as well as overcoming the bullying. They want to know how to unify their sense of home and school. They wish to understand the relevance of different parts of the curriculum together with the relevance of *how* they are working. They know, for example, that a subject like English or maths might be important, but find the way in which they work in art or science more beneficial. Out of all the contradictions children form a unified view of what school is for, and what it is like. It is a view which has a great deal of relevance to all the issues that underlie any school, from the curriculum to teacher appraisal.

Meanwhile, we seem to accept the conditions of schools without question. If there are doubts about the education system it is teachers or educationalists who are blamed. Children at school have a number of pointed comments to make which also raise issues of the relationship between education and society. Schools do not appear to have a central place in the community. Their very separateness is part of the 'hidden' curriculum, nurturing in children a clear idea of what society as a whole feels about education. But children also make us aware, whilst in school, of what they are capable of. There is a huge potential that is as yet untapped. Talking to children makes it clear that they are aware of this too.

NOTES AND REFERENCES

1. Measor, L. and Woods, P. *Changing Schools: Pupil Perspectives on Transfer to a Comprehensive*. Milton Keynes: Open University Press, 1984.

2. Bretherton, I., Fritz, J., Zahn-Waxter, C. and Ridgeway, D. 'Learning to talk about functions: a functionalist perspective.' *Child Development* **57** 529–548, 1986.

3. Horn, W. and Packard, T. ('Early identification of learning problems: a meta-analysis.' *Journal of Educational Psychology* **77** (5), 597–607, 1985) conducted a survey of 58 studies on correlations between tests in kindergarten and reading achievement later, and concluded that the best predictors of achievement were attention, the ability to internalize behaviour problems and language.

4. Eg. girls suggest higher social values and boys higher material values. Simmons, C. and Wade, W. 'Young people's least ideals in five countries.' *Educational Review* **37** (3), 289–298, 1985.

5. Cullingford, C. *Parents, Teachers and Schools*. London: Robert Royce, 1985, Chapter 8.

6. Cf. Davies, B. *Life in the Classroom and Playground: The Accounts of Primary School Children*. London: Routledge and Kegan Paul, 1982.

7. E.g. Ghaye, A. 'Outer appearances with inner experience: towards a more holistic view of group work.' *Educational Review* **38** (1), 45–56, 1986.

8. Measor and Woods, *op.cit.*, pp 105–110.

9. Technology is a good example of this, Once part of craft and design, then allied to science, technology has been given such status that it is a subject seen by its advocates to embrace all others.

10. Goodnow, J. and Burns, A. *Home and School: A Child's Eye View*. London: Allen and Unwin, 1985.

11. Cf. Bronfenbrenner, V. *The Ecology of Human Development: Experiments of Nature and Design*, Cambridge, Mass: Harvard University Press, 1979.

12. Austin-Ward, B. 'English, English teaching and English teachers: the perceptions of 16 year olds.' *Educational Research* **28** (1), pp. 32–42, Feb. 1986.

13. Lee, P.C., Statuto, C.M. and Kedar-Voivodas, G. 'Elementary school children's perceptions of their actual and ideal school experience: a developmental study.' *Journal of Educational Psychology* **75** (6), 838–847, 1983.

14. Simmons and Wade *op.cit.*

15. White, R. with Brockington, D. *Tales out of School: Consumer's Views of British Education*. London: Routledge and Kegan Paul, 1983.

Index